Maestro Ferlingatti and his string quartet were astonished by the colorful crowd that fell from the ceiling.

The Maestro loved an audience, even if they dropped in unannounced. But when Walter's bed smashed through the floor and paint splattered everywhere, the Maestro wished his audience would leave. And so they did, along with his string quartet.

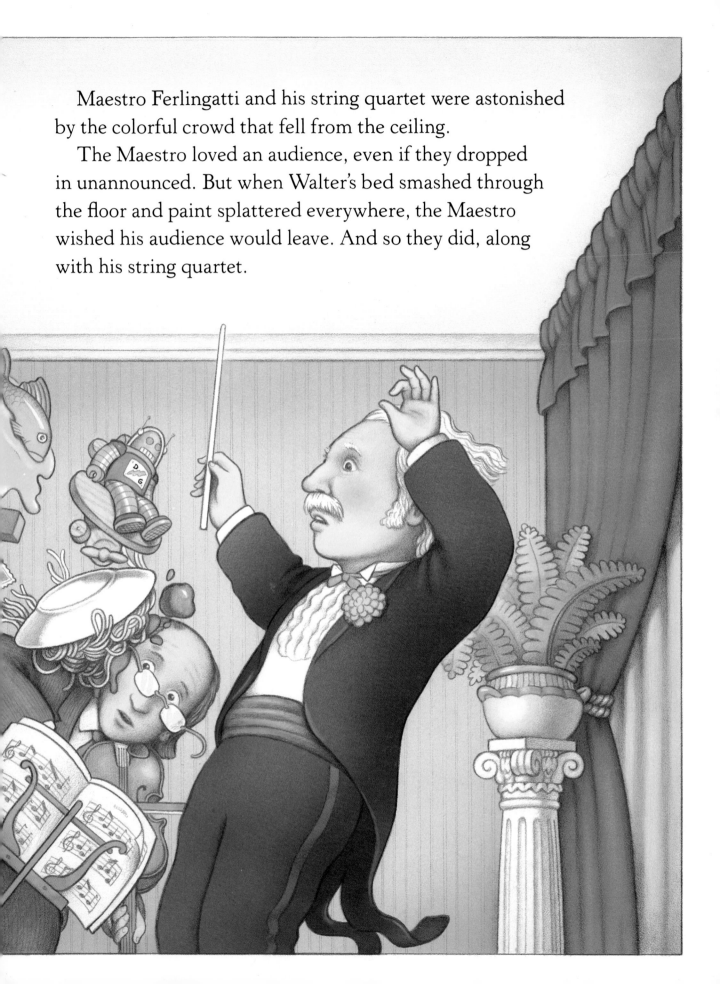

Maestro Ferlingatti's practice room floor was also the basement ceiling. It was dark and quiet as midnight down there. Walter squeezed his eyes closed and tumbled through the darkness until he landed on something soft. . . .

He opened his eyes. Everything was in its place. His bedroom lights were out. The door was almost closed and through it Walter could hear his mother and father talking quietly.

"No more jumping on the bed for me," mumbled Walter as he lay back down to sleep.

Suddenly he heard a creak, the ceiling cracked, and down came Delbert, bed and all. Down and down fell Delbert. . . .

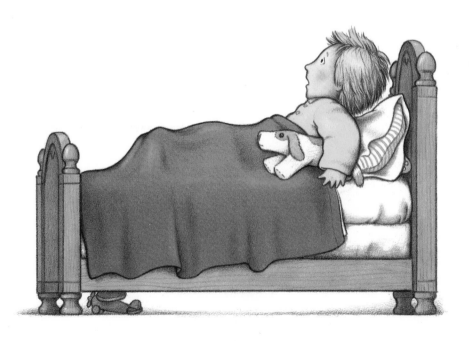

DISNEY® DOLLS

Identification & Value Guide

by Margo Rana

Published by

Hobby
House
Press

Hobby House Press, Inc.
Grantsville, MD 21536

Introduction

I have been working on this Disney project for several years. I have had more fun putting this book together than all my other books put together! I attribute my feelings for the Mattel Disney dolls mainly because the characters bring fond childhood memories. The anticipation and excitement that preceded the days that passed before I would go to the cinema on Saturday morning to see Sleeping Beauty, Snow White or Cinderella were almost unbearable. I must have driven my parents nuts! I sense that you and I have a bond brought together through the dolls that have been created for us by Disney and Mattel. Playing "Disney Doll" with my friends and associates is always the highlight of my day. I would like to thank them for both playing, helping and working with me on this and other projects. They are; Robert Gardner, Michelle Walker, Carolyn Klemovec, Joan Mitchell, and Pat Slack Sethney. I would also like to thank Roger Gerdes for his friendship and legal assistance in regard to this and my previous four books.

I would like to take this opportunity to clarify one Mattel/Disney category. The term Disney Classics is one that Mattel assigned the early Disney Dolls. Only those dolls, which have the term "Classics" printed on the box, are in fact Disney Classics. All others have a different classification. Each chapter in this book is introduced by the collection and should so be noted. The prices are a guide and are not set in stone. I have opted to give you a range that you might expect to pay for the dolls or fashions. The differences in the prices could be supply and demand for a particular part of the country or as simple as box condition. If you are a box collector you will want to make it your responsibility to inquire about the condition of the box.

Exclusively yours,
Margo Rana

Additional copies of this book may be purchased at $24.95 (plus postage and handling) from

HOBBY HOUSE PRESS, INC.

1 Corporate Drive
Grantsville, Maryland 21536

1-800-554-1447

or from Margo's 2726 De la Vina Street, Santa Barbara, CA 93105 Fax 805-563-0124
or from your favorite bookstore or dealer.

©1999 by Margo Rana

ISBN: 0-87588-541-1

Table of Contents

Beauty & the Beast
Beast

Cinderella
Cinderella

Aladdin
Jasmine

Hercules
Hercules

Snow White & the
Seven Dwarfs
Snow White

The Hunchback of
Notre Dame
Quasimodo

Sleeping Beauty
Aurora

Pocahontas
Pocahontas

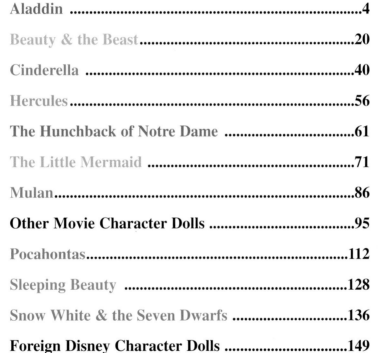

Mulan
Mulan

The Little Mermaid
Ariel

Disney characters © Disney Enterprises, Inc.

Disney characters © Disney Enterprises, Inc.

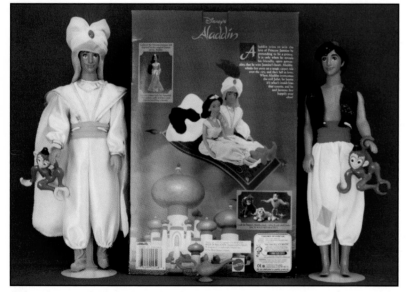

Disney characters © Disney Enterprises, Inc.

Disney's Aladdin
#2548 • 1992 • $35-40

Aladdin doll is packaged as a gift set. *Aladdin* comes with an extra fashion. Dress your doll in the two piece ensemble on the left and *Aladdin* is instantly converted into the handsome *Prince Ali*. His vest is made of purple suede cloth and is sprinkled with gold pixie dust. His white pants with a gold colored patch sewn at the knee are nylon. There is a built-in red cummerbund at the waist. The *Prince*'s two-piece ensemble appears to be acetate and is trimmed with gold lamé at the neck and wrists. The cape he is wearing is sprinkled with pixie dust and wraps at the waist with the gold cummerbund that matches the patch on his other pants. The *Prince*'s turban is made of nylon chiffon and has a lilac colored tuft with a matching plastic jewel in the center. His slip-on boots are made of doe-colored suede cloth. *Aladdin*'s lamp in the first releases changed color from tan to yellow; later releases were not color changeable. The hands on "Abu" were painted flesh color in the beginning. Soon after the dolls hit the store shelves, Mattel stopped painting them. There is speculation that this was ceased to save money. The doll is stamped ©1968 Mattel Inc. This date does not have anything to do with the date that the doll was available for purchase. The dates on the dolls are the patent date. The doll in this photo was made in Malaysia.

ALADDIN

Disney's Aladdin
Jasmine
#2557 • 1992 • $35-40

Aladdin *Jasmine* doll comes as a gift set with an extra fashion. *Jasmine's* two piece nylon aqua day-dress is secured with Velcro™. It is unfortunate because the Velcro™ grabs the doll's hair and clothes causing considerable damage. Her fashion is sprinkled with golden "pixie dust." She has a plastic aquamarine jewel headband on a matching satin ribbon. Her gold colored collar necklace fastens at the back. The second fashion is known as "*Jasmine's* Palace Outfit." The one-piece lilac nylon dress has an overlay skirt of fragile chiffon spattered with pixie dust and with long chiffon sleeves. The portrait collar is made of iridescent fabric with gold tone thread to match her separate overskirt. Included with the ensemble is a matching lilac headband with plastic jewel. (Not shown). *Jasmine's* large earrings are molded. The doll in this photo was made in China.

Disney characters © Disney Enterprises, Inc.

Disney characters © Disney Enterprises, Inc.

Disney characters © Disney Enterprises, Inc.

ALADDIN

Disney characters © Disney
Enterprises, Inc.

Disney characters © Disney Enterprises, Inc.

Disney characters © Disney Enterprises, Inc.

Disney's Aladdin
Jasmine's Evening Palace Gown
#10589 • 1993 • $18-22

Jasmine's "Evening Palace Gown" two piece ensemble is a strapless empire style gown. The top is gold lamé with a chiffon overlay with gold tone "pixie dust." Her hooded cape is one of the most delicate fashions in the collection. It is trimmed with gold tone thread and a tie ribbon closure. Included in the flat pack is a necklace that is extremely similar to the dressed box doll's, but it is not exact, it is slightly larger. There is a separate matching rose-colored headpiece. The fashion in this photo was made in China.

Disney's Aladdin
Jasmine's Traveling Coat
#10588 • 1993 • $18-22

Jasmine's "Traveling Coat" ensemble is a rich deep peacock blue becoming of a Princess. The collar is iridescent and the body of the coat is sprinkled with swirls of gold to accent the gold lamé trim all around the coat. Underneath, *Jasmine* wears a two-piece harem fashion. The bandeau top is made from the same fabric as her coat. The pants have built-in panties with a waistband to match the doll's necklace. The pant legs are a delicate chiffon with elastic at the ankles. The bronze tone shoes with turned up toes are a first for Mattel. This mold to date is exclusive to *Jasmine*. Both this fashion and "Evening Palace Gown" fashion were sold in flat packs. The bottom of the package is a magic carpet and is fun to display the dolls on. The fashion in this photo was made in China.

6

ALADDIN

Disney's Aladdin
Jasmine Gift Pack
No stock # • No date • $150

Jasmine Gift Pack is one of the two most rare items from any of the Disney doll series. The other will be covered in the chapter on *Cinderella*. There is no stock number assigned to this item. There is speculation that this gift set was possibly a promotional item that Mattel had made up for marketing the doll and fashion. There is no confirmation or denial from either Disney or Mattel. It seems to be a mystery item. The gift pack includes a packaged *Jasmine* and her two fashions mounted on thick cardboard. Purchasing the three items on the board separately will result in savings, but this is truly the one to own. The fashions and doll in this gift pack were made in China.

Disney characters © Disney Enterprises, Inc.

Disney characters © Disney Enterprises, Inc.

Disney's Aladdin
Magic Carpet Gift Set
#10657 • 1993 • $60-70

Magic Carpet Gift Set's uniqueness is in the carpet. The happy couple flies off into the night while the magical carpet plays the melody "A Whole New World." The batteries are non-replaceable; therefore your carpet might not play a tune. *Aladdin* doll's two piece costume accents *Jasmine*'s perfectly. His grape colored coat with soft pink-collar matches his one-piece jumpsuit. The turned up toes on the gold lamé boots are made from the same trim you see on his coat. *Aladdin*'s matching molded hat really tops it all off. *Jasmine* doll's four-piece

Disney characters © Disney Enterprises, Inc.

fashion is extremely delicate and is subject to extreme picking as a result of so many Velcro™ closures at the back. The tricot bodice has a portrait collar of iridescent fabric and grape colored chiffon sleeves. Her harem pants are solid, while her separate overskirt and matching chiffon stole are sprinkled with "pixie dust." Both dolls in this photo were made in China.

ALADDIN

Disney's Aladdin
Water Jewel Magic Aladdin
#11273 • 1993 • $12-18

Water Jewel Magic Aladdin doll wears a two piece swim set. His vest is regal purple suede cloth with gold tone trim. His swim trunks are made of polyester with gold lamé trim. The wide gold lamé waistband with an amethyst colored plastic stone is made from the same fabric as Mattel's 1994 Happy Holiday doll. This same fabric has been used on innumerable Mattel dolls over the years. Warm water makes the stone turn to pink. Cold water makes it turn to amethyst again. The box you see in this photo was from Europe and was called Jewel Magic. The American version had the same stock number. The doll in this photo was made in China.

Disney's Aladdin
Water Jewel Magic Jasmine
#11272 • 1993 • $12-18

Water Jewel Magic Jasmine doll wears a gold and purple lamé one-piece swimsuit. She has a matching detachable overskirt with purple suede cloth trim. Included with this doll are a hair decoration and a hairbrush. The jewel on *Jasmine's* swimsuit changes colors when submerged in water just like *Aladdin's*. The doll in this photo was made in China.

Disney characters © Disney Enterprises, Inc.

Disney characters © Disney Enterprises, Inc.

Disney characters © Disney Enterprises, Inc.

Disney's Aladdin
Water Surprise Aladdin
#12641 • 1994 • $12-18

Water Surprise Aladdin doll is wearing a cheerful two piece outfit. The metallic blue and green in his vest and shorts are perfect for the warm pools of the oasis. *Aladdin* has a magic lamp with jewel around his neck, which opens and closes. It hangs from a fine black cord. His pants change color in warm water. The doll in this photo was made in China. *Doll courtesy of Michelle Walker.*

Disney's Aladdin
Water Surprise Jasmine
#12640 • 1994 • $12-18

Water Surprise Jasmine doll's outfit is a metallic two-piece swimsuit. Part of the swimsuit changes color in warm water. She has a waterlily flower on her wrist, that opens and closes in warm/cold water which has a blue plastic jewel in the center. The doll in this photo was made in China. *Doll courtesy of Michelle Walker.*

Disney characters © Disney Enterprises, Inc.

Disney's Aladdin
Jasmine & Rajah Friendship Gift Set • #10587 • 1993 • $55-65

Jasmine gift set doll is a wearing a gorgeous buttercup colored two-piece fashion. *Jasmine's* bandeau top has an orange plastic jewel, which matches the one on her headband. Her matching pants and chiffon veil are loaded with pixie dust. The harem shoes match her orange molded earrings. The orange bracelet is a jelly bracelet like Mattel first included with their "Wet 'n Wild" dolls from 1989. From head to waist Mattel utilizes wonderful iridescent vinyl on *Jasmine's* headband, necklace and waistband. Included in this wonderful gift set is *Jasmine's* loyal companion "Rajah." He is a large handsome stuffed tiger with fabulous faux fur mane. The doll in this photo was made in China.

Disney characters © Disney Enterprises, Inc.

ALADDIN

Disney characters © Disney Enterprises, Inc.

Disney's Aladdin
Water Jewel Magic Gift Set • #11769 • 1994 • $85-95

Water Jewel Magic Gift Set is extremely hard to find. It was a Disneyland and Disney World exclusive. The package includes *Water Jewel Aladdin* and *Jasmine* and "Rajah" dolls. This is the same "Rajah," which was included in the *Jasmine & "Rajah" Friendship Gift Set* on page 10). Although the doll's jewels change colors when dipped in the pool, "Rajah" does not change colors and should not be submerged in water. The dolls in this gift set were made in China. *Gift set courtesy of Christine Fuscaldo.*

Disney characters © Disney Enterprises, Inc.

ALADDIN

Disney's Aladdin
Genie of the Lamp • #5305 • No box date • $20-25

Genie of the Lamp doll has a hard plastic head with a soft body, legs and arms. I vaguely remember seeing these sets at one of the bigger toy chains. I don't know why I didn't buy it. It is much cuter than I remembered first seeing it. You can stuff your *Genie* into the lamp as seen on the back of the box. The doll in this photo was made by Arcotoys, Inc., a Mattel Company in China. *Doll courtesy of Michelle Walker.*

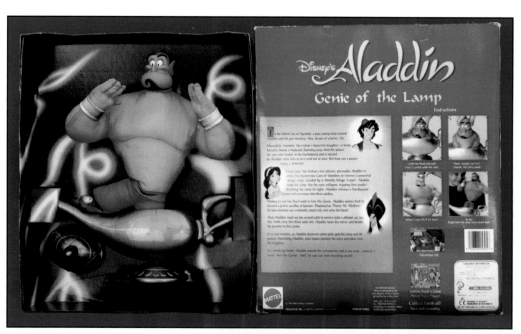

ALADDIN

Disney characters © Disney Enterprises, Inc.

Disney's Aladdin
Tourist Genie
#5340 • No box date • $25-35

Tourist Genie figure comes with a brightly colored Hawaiian print shirt and solid yellow shorts. There are two orange golf clubs, golf bag and a cap made of plastic that is *Goofy*'s face. The doll in this photo was made by Arcotoys, Inc., a Mattel Company in China.

Disney characters © Disney Enterprises, Inc.

Disney characters © Disney Enterprises, Inc.

Disney's Aladdin
Fashion Genie
#10709 • 1993 • $25-30

Fashion Genie doll looks very similar to the previous one. His body is part plastic and part cloth. He comes with a yellow and rose pink shirt a tuxedo dickey, and a *Goofy* hat. The doll in this photo was made in China.

Disney characters © Disney Enterprises, Inc.

13

Disney's Aladdin
Special Sparkles Jasmine
#11922 • 1994 • $20-40

Special Sparkles Jasmine doll has eyes that reflect light, which causes the doll's eyes to sparkle at you. Her eyes are not the only things to sparkle. Her costume from head to toe is loaded with glitter. The chiffon is a bit stiff. I attribute this to the glue, which adheres to the tiny flakes of glitter. Her faux jewel tiara and necklace and removable gold tone earrings, ring and shoes are made from hard metallic plastic. This is the first *Jasmine* doll to have removable earrings. The doll in this photo was made in China.

Disney characters © Disney Enterprises, Inc.

Disney characters © Disney Enterprises, Inc.

Disney's Aladdin
Arabian Lights Jasmine
#11750 • 1994 • $20-30

Arabian Lights Jasmine doll's ensemble is the only red fashion *Jasmine* has to date. It is a fine color choice for the only red-lipped *Jasmine* doll in the collection. Also unique to this doll are the flashing ruby-red earrings and headpiece. This is the first *Jasmine* doll to sport a detachable ring in her finger. The doll is equipped with batteries and an automatic shut off switch. This is a unique feature, which will allow longer life for the replaceable batteries. Her gently embossed gold lamé bandeau top matches the skirt's waistband. The bloomer tricot pants with an attached overskirt are decorated with stars and crescent moons that glow in the dark. *Arabian Lights Jasmine* has long pitch-black hair that is woven with colorful hair twists. Naturally, she comes with her own hairbrush. The doll in this photo was made in China.

Disney characters © Disney Enterprises, Inc.

ALADDIN

Disney characters © Disney Enterprises, Inc.

Disney's Aladdin
Fantasy Hair Jasmine
#13126 • 1994 • $20-30

Fantasy Hair Jasmine doll is wearing a three-piece costume, which truly accents her pitch-black hair. The bandeau top is trimmed with gold lamé and purple satin. Her solid petal pink pants are topped with a regal purple skirt with glitter gold mosaic pattern. The pink harem shoes are a perfect match. The exciting feature of this doll is her floor length hair. It can be styled with her gold tone corded hair trim with wire running through it for special styling techniques. Included in the doll's package are hot pink shoes and a plastic hairbrush to help with the styling. The doll in this photo was made in China.

Disney characters © Disney Enterprises, Inc.

Disney's Aladdin & the
King of Thieves
Princess in Pink Jasmine
#16200 • 1996 • $40-45

Princess in Pink Jasmine doll is wearing a two-piece fashion of deep rose pink tricot with chiffon sleeves and pant overlay. This is the only *Jasmine* doll to have a hat. Her gold colored shoes accent her molded earrings and plastic necklace. Included with this doll, but not listed on the box is a hot pink hairbrush. *Princess in Pink Jasmine* is hard to find. The doll in this photo was made in China.

Disney characters © Disney Enterprises, Inc.

Disney characters © Disney Enterprises, Inc.

Disney's Aladdin and the King of Theives
Palace Wedding Jasmine
#16199 • 1996 • $20-30

Palace Wedding Jasmine doll is extremely rare. I thought I was never going to get one. There had been reported that Mattel was to have made a *Wedding Palace Gift* set, stock number was #15822 but I have yet to see one. *Jasmine's* modest wedding gown is made from white tricot. It has the same gold lamé fabric as seen on several other dolls. Her veil is rather plain with a few heavily glittered flowers. Her harem shoes removable wedding ring and hairbrush are white plastic. The doll in this photo was made in China.

Disney characters © Disney Enterprises, Inc.

Disney characters © Disney Enterprises, Inc.

Palace Wedding Gift Set • #15822 • 1996 • $N/A

Pictured on the back of *Palace Wedding Jasmine* doll's box is *Aladdin*. This was supposed to have been a gift set, however it was never released into the market place.

Disney characters © Disney Enterprises, Inc.

Disney's Aladdin
Princess Stories Collection Jasmine
#18191 • 1997 • $25-30

Princess Stories Collection Jasmine doll's lavender tricot ensemble is fabulous with her skin tone. In fact, *Jasmine* looks amazingly wonderful in pastels as well as jewel tones. This is an unusual ability. Her tricot top, pants and overskirt with chiffon trim are simple yet flattering. She is adorned with three jewels one on her headband and hard plastic choker. Her harem shoes are dyed to match. *Jasmine* comes with two palace doves and a Little Little Golden Book. The doll in this photo was made in China.

Disney characters © Disney Enterprises, Inc.

ALADDIN

Disney's Aladdin
Dress-Up Dream™ Jasmine • #20421 • 1998 • $25-30

Dress-Up Dream Jasmine doll is a dream come true, especially for little girls to play with. She is wearing a nylon jade green harem outfit. The shoulders, midriff, waist, chiffon pant legs and ankles are trimmed with golden leatherette. There are twenty plastic jewels that easily hook on to her costume to dress it up. Adorning her hair is a golden band with a plastic ruby jewel and two gold lamé ribbons. Her choker is gold plastic with an amethyst color plastic jewel. Included in the package is a grape colored sachet bag with a gold ribbon drawstring like the ones in her hair. You get three chipboard clip art characters, a purple hairbrush and a pair of jade green harem shoes. The doll in this photo was made in China.

Disney characters © Disney Enterprises, Inc.

Disney characters © Disney Enterprises, Inc.

Disney characters © Disney Enterprises, Inc.

Disney's Beauty and the Beast
Disney's Classics Belle
#2433 • 1991 • $60-75

Disney Classics *Belle* doll was first manufactured with bangs and the second issue was made without bangs. The later is referred to as "No-bang Belle." Both dolls have the same stock number, same packaging and the same accessories. *Belle's* golden ball gown has a "pixie dusted" chiffon overskirt with sleeves to match. Her gauntlets match her dress and shoes. This wonderful gift set comes with a separate blue dress with a white apron with pixie dust printed on it. It comes with a separate hair ribbon and matching blue shoes. As an extra bonus you get two pop-up characters. Included in early releases was a tube of lipstick. The doll in this photo was made in China.

BEAUTY & THE BEAST

Disney characters © Disney Enterprises, Inc.

Disney characters © Disney Enterprises, Inc.

Disney characters © Disney Enterprises, Inc.

Disney's Beauty and the Beast
Disney Classics The Beast
#2436 • 1992 • $60-75

The Beast doll was boxed as a gift set. The Prince's rooted hair makes him particularly handsome. His fashion appears to be several pieces but it is actually a one-piece jumpsuit. His jabot, vest, knickers and socks are all stitched together. He wears black plastic slip on loafers. The *Beast's* costume is not the first that Mattel made with a mask. The concept was introduced in 1964, when Mattel made a Little Theater costume called "Little Red Riding Hood and the Wolf." The mask slips easily over the head of any 12-inch figure. I chose an old suntanned *Malibu Ken* doll because the color of his chest matched the coloring in the *Beast's* mask so well. The *Beast's* jacket is made of royal blue felt with gold lamé trim fabric to match *Belle's* ball gown. The black nylon knickers appear to be separate but they are actually attached to his feet. The same is true with his paws. It does not show well in the photograph, but he actually has dark brown felt claws. He looks a bit gruff, but underneath he is quite a debonair Prince. Included in this set are a comb, a brush, a faux mirror and two pop-up characters. The doll in this photo was made in Malaysia.

BEAUTY & THE BEAST

Disney's Beauty and the Beast
Disney Classics Winter Belle
#1637 • 1992 • $110-150

Disney Classic *Winter Belle* doll is one of the most popular dolls and one of the hardest to find that Mattel has made for Disney. The doll and ball gown are identical to the doll and fashion found in the Beauty and the Beast Gift Set. (See page 23.) The uniqueness of this doll is the cape she is wearing. Most of Mattel's fur-trimmed fashions are amongst collector favorites. *Belle's* cape is exclusive to this gift set. She comes with a wrist-rose, hairbrush and pink pearl shoes. Included are two plastic characters they are "Mrs. Potts" and "Chip." There is also a Little Little Golden Book. The doll in this photo was made in China.

Disney characters © Disney Enterprises, Inc.

Disney characters © Disney Enterprises, Inc.

Disney characters © Disney Enterprises, Inc.

Disney's Beauty and the Beast
Disney Classics Belle and the Beast
Gift Set
#1622 • 1992 • $120-135

Disney Classics *Belle* doll in this gift set and Disney *Classics Winter Belle* are both "No-bang" dolls. The bodice of her gown is rose pink and the skirt is pale pink with glittery "fairy dust" and is trimmed with an even paler pink satin ribbon. She has pearl-pink pumps and a wrist rose just like *Winter Belle*. There is a hairbrush included in the package. The *Beast's* mask looks the same as in the original, however, The Beast's mane is lighter in color. *Beast's* outfit is extremely similar to the original Beast's gift set. The major difference is the color of his jacket, which in this set is turquoise. His bottoms look like pants but he is actually wearing a one-piece jumpsuit. The doll in this photo was made in Malaysia.

BEAUTY & THE BEAST

Beauty and the Beast
Disney Classsics Dinner Fashion
#3152 • 1992 • $35-40

Belle in Disney's *Beauty and the Beast* feature film had many wardrobe changes. Mattel recreated her entire wardrobe. The lavender dress seen in the photo is the fashion that *Belle* wore to the dinner party. The white apron is sprinkled with "pixie dust." This fashion has been found with either a pale pink or a lavender hair ribbon and matching lavender shoes. The accessories included in this flat pack are four sets of dishes, forks, knives and spoons. There are two pink napkins with gold braiding, napkin holders and a feather-duster pop-up character. The plastic dinnerware was made in Italy. The doll in this photo was made in China.

BEAUTY & THE BEAST

Beauty and the Beast
Disney Classics Dinner Fashion
#3153 • 1992 •$35-40

Disney Classics *Belle* doll's "Library Fashion" is special and very feminine. The bodice is tricot with "pixie dust" and the skirt is iridescent. Her leg-a-mutton sleeves are iridescent and chiffon which softens the gown nicely. *Belle* has a straw bag to carry an assortment of imitation books. Included in the package is a matching green satin ribbon for her hair and a matching pair of closed-toe pumps. Also included is a footstool pop-up character. The fashion in this photo was made in China.

Disney characters © Disney Enterprises, Inc.

Disney characters © Disney Enterprises, Inc.

Disney's Beauty and the Beast
Disney Classics Village Belle
#1647 • 1992 • $45-55

Disney Classics *Village Belle* doll comes in a slim-line box. Her one-piece dress is very simple and has matching pixie dust as on her detachable apron. Included in the package are a blue satin hair ribbon and blue close-toe pumps. The *Village Belle* seen here has no bangs. Some Village Belle boxes have been found with *Be Our Guest Musical Belle* dolls in the packages. You can see that the *Be Our Guest* doll has different face paint and bangs. The doll in this photo was made in China.

Disney characters © Disney Enterprises, Inc.

BEAUTY & THE BEAST

Disney's Beauty and the Beast
Disney Classics Be Our Guest Musical Gift Set
#10477 • 1993 • $145-155

Disney Classics *Be Our Guest Musical Belle* doll is wearing a village dress. You saw on previous pages two other versions. This one is the more elaborate version. Mattel chose a more expensive satin fabric for the jumper with tricot for the sleeves and bodice. Even her blue and silver lamé hair ribbon is more elegant. *Belle's* table has a special feature that had never been used before. Not only does the table play "Be Our Guest" but it turns also. The only unfortunate thing is that if you have the table set, sometimes the accessories fall off while the table turns. This set comes with the following plastic figures: "Lumiere," "Cogsworth," "Mrs. Potts," and "Chip." The table setting includes four napkins, four glasses, four plates, four spoons and four knives. In addition to the *Belle* doll and fashion you get a hair brush and matching blue shoes. The doll in this photo was made in China.

Disney characters © Disney Enterprises, Inc.

Disney characters © Disney Enterprises, Inc.

Disney's Beauty and the Beast
Disney Classics Be Our Guest Musical Table Gift Set
#10571 • 1993 • $40-50

The table, chair and accessories you see in the *Be Our Guest Musical Table Gift Set* (above) was sold without the *Belle* doll. The only way to get this doll was to purchase the *Be Our Guest Musical Table Gift Set*.

Disney characters © Disney Enterprises, Inc.

BEAUTY & THE BEAST

Disney characters © Disney Enterprises, Inc.

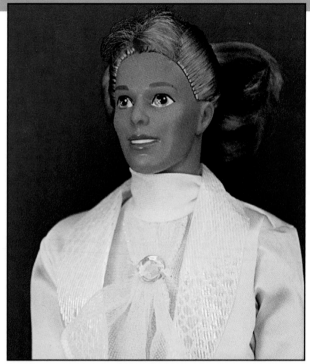

Disney characters © Disney Enterprises, Inc.

Disney characters © Disney Enterprises, Inc.

Disney characters © Disney Enterprises, Inc.

Disney's Beauty and the Beast
Wedding Musical Belle
#10909 • 1996 • $35-45

Wedding Belle doll's accessories include her musical wedding gown (see *Beauty and the Beast* Wedding Gift Set), veil, rose bouquet, white shoes and a hairbrush. Included with the doll, but not listed on the package is a white plastic wedding ring. The doll in this photo was made in China.

Disney's Beauty and the Beast
The Wedding, The Prince
#10910 • 1993 • $35-45

Wedding Prince doll's accessories are his white shoes and a hairbrush. He and his fashion are the same as the *Prince* doll in the Wedding Deluxe Gift Set. The doll in this photo was made in China.

Disney's Beauty and the Beast
The Wedding Deluxe Gift Set
Musical Belle & The Prince
#11021 • 1993 • $90-100

Disney's *Beauty and the Beast Wedding Gift Set* has the same dolls, fashions and accessories as the individual Wedding dolls. *Belle's* dress is musical. Hidden in a bow at the back of her dress is a disc that contains non-replaceable batteries. When you press on the disc it plays "Here comes the Bride" and the "Wedding Recession." The chiffon neckline is decorated with a plastic jewel. The bodice is iridescent to match the three bows on her skirt, her bouquet and on the headpiece of her tulle veil. The skirt is voluptuous white satin with a chiffon overlay. Her shoes are white plastic closed-toe pumps with molded bows. The *Belle* doll in this photo was made in China. *Beauty and the Beast Wedding Prince* is wearing a sleeveless jumpsuit with attached socks of tricot and a built in jabot. His tuxedo jacket is satin with iridescent color and cuffs to match *Belle's* gown. His shoes are white slip-ons. The *Prince* doll in this photo was made in Malaysia.

Disney characters © Disney Enterprises, Inc.

Disney characters © Disney Enterprises, Inc.

Disney characters © Disney Enterprises, Inc.

Disney characters © Disney Enterprises, Inc.

BEAUTY & THE BEAST

Disney's Beauty and the Beast
Applause Belle
#45536 • No box date • $50-60

The *Applause Belle* doll is one of my favorite *Belle* dolls for several reasons. The main reason is the packaging. I really appreciate a doll that is presented in the shoebox style. What makes *Belle's* box especially wonderful is that it has a window so you can see your doll. You can take her out and put her back in, and she stays dust free. You can flip the lid, keeping your doll in the box and take up a fraction of the space because you do not have to store the box. *Belle's* dress is as elegant as *Belle's* library fashion. It is made of the same iridescent fabric. The only accessories with this doll are a yellow hair ribbon and yellow hairbrush and yellow shoes. The doll in this photo was made by Mattel in China.

Disney characters © Disney Enterprises, Inc.

Disney's Beauty and the Beast
Applause Beast
#45239 • No Date, No Box • $40-50

The *Applause Beast* doll did not come with a box. Applause sent the *Beast* to the stores in clear plastic bags. His face hands and feet are plastic while his body is stuffed. He has a full faux fur mane and tail. He is extremely well constructed. The doll in this photo was made in China.

BEAUTY & THE BEAST

Disney's Beauty and the Beast
Special Sparkles Belle
#11923 • 1994 • $65-85

Special Sparkles Belle doll is exactly what her name suggests. This "No-Bang" *Belle* doll is special and her eyes do sparkle. Her gown is a shimmery gold metalic with matching gauntlets. The shoulders are made with iridescent fabric to match the peplum. *Belle's* jewelry includes a choker, gold tone earrings and accenting finger ring. The shoes are gold tone closed-toe pumps. The golden ribbon at the top of her head holds back her hair so that you can see her twinkling eyes. The doll in this photo was made in China. *Doll courtesy of Michelle Walker.*

Disney characters © Disney Enterprises, Inc.

Disney characters © Disney Enterprises, Inc.

Disney characters © Disney Enterprises, Inc.

Disney's Beauty and the Beast
Signature Collection Belle
Collector Edition
#16089 • 1996 • $95-105

Signature Collection Belle doll is the first doll that Mattel made for Disney in the collector division. In my opinion, she is the best made and the most elaborate of the *Belle* dolls - from her portrait neckline to the tip of her toes. The bodice is overlaid with golden crochet. The drop waist begins with gold lamé and turns to satin and chiffon. The puckering adds a fullness to the skirt that had never been done before. This is the first *Belle* doll to have earrings. They are gold-tone drops, which match her ring. *Belle* has elastic pull-on yellow bloomers underneath it all. Her gown has a snap closure back and a "Disney Collector" label sewn in the skirt. The other accessories are her golden gauntlets and special hair holder and hairbrush. *Signature Collection Belle* was the first red-lipped *Belle* doll.

Disney characters © Disney Enterprises, Inc.

The box is a work of art. The iridescent packaging is a blue on blue embossed pattern. The liner is metallic gold and enhances *Belle's* beauty. Although I would have preferred a shoebox, it is appropriate that *Belle* should have a book box. The inside cover has a pop out of Belle and the Beast dancing in the ballroom. This has to be an all-time favorite for collectors. The doll in this photo was made in Indonesia.

Disney characters © Disney Enterprises, Inc.

BEAUTY & THE BEAST

Disney characters © Disney Enterprises, Inc.

Disney characters © Disney Enterprises, Inc.

Disney's Beauty and the Beast
Signature Collection Beast
Limited Edition
#17826 • 1997 • $145-150

Signature Collection Beast doll was originally planned as the first in the Great Heroes collection but instead he was incorporated into the Signature Collection. Mattel selected the highest quality fabrics for this doll. His tuxedo jacket is the richest royal blue trimmed with the same gold lamé as in *Belle's* dress. His vest is also gold lamé and this fabric has been found on innumerable *BARBIE®* dolls and Fashion Avenue outfits. His faux fur mane is impeccably coifed. The sapphire plastic tie clip in his ascot is well positioned. The packaging has all the amenities as *Belle's*. The doll in this photo was made in China.

Disney characters © Disney Enterprises, Inc.

33

Disney characters © Disney Enterprises, Inc.

Disney's Beauty and the Beast Princess Stories Collection Belle
#18193 • 1997 • $22-30

Princess Stories Collection Belle doll was and still is a genuine value. *Belle's* fashion is made with three different fabrics. The bodice of the dress is the same fabric that we saw on the *Applause Belle* doll. The portrait collar is goldenrod chiffon with a gold bead in the center to match her earrings with slightly smaller beads on the flounce on her skirt. Her hair ribbon is also goldenrod chiffon. The skirt is suckered nylon with a built in illusion crinoline with a white nylon flounce. *Princess Stories Belle* comes with a "Lumiere" plastic figurine and a Little Little Golden Book, *Beauty and the Beast*, which was printed in the U.S.A. The doll in this photo was made in China.

Disney characters © Disney Enterprises, Inc.

Disney characters © Disney Enterprises, Inc.

BEAUTY & THE BEAST

Disney characters © Disney Enterprises, Inc.

Disney characters © Disney Enterprises, Inc.

Disney's Beauty and the Beast Dress-Up Dream™ Belle
#20420 • 1998 • $15-20

Dress-Up Dream Belle, doll to date is the hardest of the three dolls in the series to find. Although Mattel assigned *Belle*, *Cinderella* and *Jasmine Dress-Up Dream* dolls their own stock number, the dolls were actually sold as an assortment. The first assortments were delivered to the shops without *Belle* in the shipping cartons. *Belle's* golden shimmering gown is trimmed with gold-tone netting. There are ten satin rosettes with pale green satin ribbon that look like stems, which can be slipped through the netting to decorate her dress. Her jewelry is limited to plastic gold stud earrings. Her accessories include a drawstring bag from the same fabric as her dress, a yellow hairbrush and yellow shoes. There is punch-out clip art of "Mrs. Potts," "Chip" and "Lumiere." The doll in this photo was made in China.

Disney characters © Disney Enterprises, Inc.

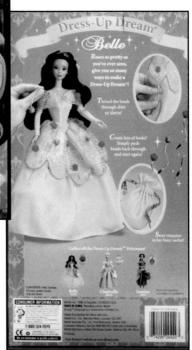

Disney characters © Disney Enterprises, Inc.

Disney characters © Disney Enterprises, Inc.

Disney characters © Disney Enterprises, Inc.

Disney characters © Disney
Enterprises, Inc.

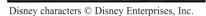

Disney characters © Disney Enterprises, Inc.

Disney's Beauty and the Beast Holiday Princess Collection Belle Special Edition
#16710 • 1997 • $40-45

THE *Enchanted Christmas Belle* doll is from the "Holiday Princess Collection." *Belle's* holiday gown has a satin bodice with a white and gold brocade insert. It has three-quarter satin sleeves with gold braid and chiffon sleeves with delicate bow and satin rosette. Her full skirt is rich burgundy crushed velveteen with an insert of white and gold brocade as in the bust line. There is a large gold lamé bow at the back of her dress to match the ribbon in her hair. Her earrings are gold drop earrings and she has matching shoes. The doll in this photo was made in Malaysia.

Disney's Beauty and the Beast
Winter Dreams Belle
Disney Special Edition
#19845 • 1998 • $40-75

Winter Dreams Belle doll was an exclusive Special Edition for K B Toys. As you can see, *Belle* has a new coif. This is the first time that we have seen *Belle* with ringlets. This is the second Disney exclusive doll for K B Toys; the first in the series was *Winter Dreams Cinderella*. The first one included a signature saddle stand; this package does not have one in it. *Belle's* gown is amazingly soft and feminine. The fabric selection is fabulous together. The shoulders of the gown are made of the airiest white chiffon, which agrees with the peplum. The peplum is garnished with clusters or miniature gold-tone rosettes while the portrait collar has a white chiffon bow accented with gold-tone trim and three golden beads. The bodice is red satin and velvet and the skirt is poinsettia red and has a red net crinoline. *Belle's* accessories include long white gloves, a white faux fur headband and a white faux fur muff; this definitely enhances her femininity. Her jewelry includes gold-tone plastic rose-stud earrings with faux pearl drops, a matching faux pearl and bead choker and a matching ring. The shoes are red closed-toe pumps and have also been found with red chunky shoe-boots. There is a white plastic hairbrush included in this remarkable package. The doll in this photo was made in Malaysia.

Disney's Beauty and the Beast
THE Enchanted Christmas Belle
#19701 • 1998 • $15-30

This *Belle* doll from WalMart is wearing her wintry fashion from the video *THE Enchanted Christmas*. Her holly-green dress is trimmed with fur at the neck, cuffs and drop waist. Her only accessories are a pair of gold-tone stud earrings and a pair of white ice skates with gray blades. Included in the box is a hairbrush. The doll in this photo was made in Indonesia.

Disney characters © Disney Enterprises, Inc.

Disney characters © Disney Enterprises, Inc.

Disney characters © Disney Enterprises, Inc.

Disney's Beauty and the Beast
Beauty and the Beast Fantasy Playset • #81205 • 1992 • $35-45

Jantex made this incredible doll carry case. It is extremely compact and allows collectors and children alike, to have lots of fun displaying their dolls. It opens and closes easily and dolls and fashions can be neatly stored away. A similar style case was also available for *Snow White* and *Pocahontas*. Dolls and figurines not included, display only.

Disney characters © Disney Enterprises, Inc.

CINDERELLA

Disney characters © Disney Enterprises, Inc.

Disney characters © Disney Enterprises, Inc.

Disney characters © Disney Enterprises, Inc.

Disney Classics Cinderella
Cinderella
#1624 • 1991 • $50-60

Disney Classics *Cinderella* doll is one of my favorites, probably more for the accessories that were sold separately than for the doll itself. You will see more on the props later in this chapter. *Cinderella's* ball gown is multi layered. She has a white satin-finished body suit with full puff sleeves. She comes with a blue satin sleeveless vest that slips over the body suit and is worn with a full pixie dusted satin skirt. The skirt is reversible to white satin with a layer of chiffon. Once you have removed the blue vest and reversed the skirt, *Cinderella's* ball gown becomes her magnificent wedding gown! Just add her veil and she and *Prince Charming* are off for their wedding. *Cinderella* wears a black satin ribbon choker and white gloves. Her hair is held back off her face with a wide blue satin ribbon. Her earrings are silver-tone studs. Her shoes are clear closed-toed pumps with silver glitter. Included in the early releases is a *Little Little Cinderella Golden Book*. Also included are two paper fold-back blue birds who helped sew her dress for the ball. This was the first doll that Mattel made for Disney with a special non-*BARBIE*® face mold. The doll in this photo was made in China.

CINDERELLA

Disney Classics Cinderella Prince Charming
#1625 • 1991• $75-95

Disney Classics *Prince Charming* is not only charming but extremely good-looking too. *Prince Charming's* jacket is white suede cloth, strewn golden "fairy dust," with gold braiding and looped trim on his epaulettes. His collar and cuffs are silver lamé and match the side seam of his tomato red dress pants. He carries a blue and golden satin pillow with gold threads with *Cinderella's* faux glass clear plastic slipper. Included within the package is a child's plastic locket on a blue satin ribbon and paper fold backs of the "Grand Duke," "Jaq" and "Gus," the mice. He has white nylon socks and his shoes are dress-black slip-ons. The doll in this photo was made in China.

Disney characters © Disney Enterprises, Inc.

CINDERELLA

**Disney Classics Cinderella
Fairy Godmother
Mask & Costume Playset
#2419 • 1992
Box $50-60 • Flat Pack $40-50**

Disney Classics *Fairy Godmother* costume came in either a box version or a flat pack. The early releases were in boxes. Shortly after Mattel released these in flat packs. Mattel changed the packaging almost immediately when they realized a considerable cost savings. Her gown is a one-piece sleeveless dress with a matching pink-lined sleeved cape with a moderate amount of "pixie dust" on one shoulder. The mask is attached to the cape. When you refer to the photographs you will see that *Fairy Godmother's* satin ribbon is either light or dark pink. There was no need to include a hairbrush as the hair on her mask is molded. She came with powder blue closed-toe pumps and two pop-up characters. The costume in the box version photo was made in China. The costume in the flat pack was made in China. *Boxed fashion, courtesy of Mindy Jackson.*

Disney characters © Disney Enterprises, Inc.

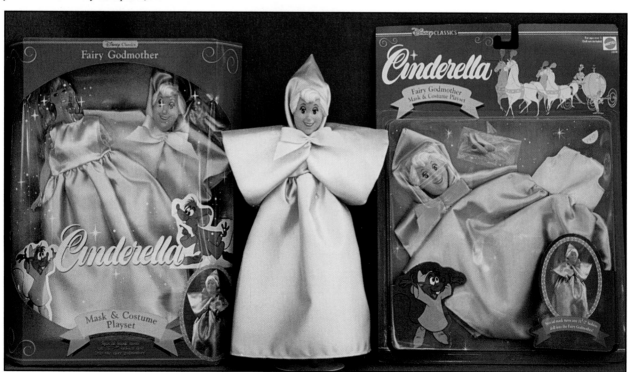

Disney characters © Disney Enterprises, Inc.

CINDERELLA

Disney Classics Cinderella Wicked Stepmother Mask & Costume Playset
#2421 • 1992
Box $50-60 • Flat Pack $40-50

Disney Classics *Wicked Stepmother's* costume, as with *Cinderella's Fairy Godmother*, had a package change immediately after initial releases into the marketplace. *Wicked Stepmother's* floor-length gown is made of rose pink satin with lavender nylon trim at the collar and cuffs. Her mask has a built-in pale lavender scarf with "pixie dust." Her facial expression is as wicked as her intentions to destroy *Cinderella's* opportunity to be the next princess. She wears black closed-toe shoes. Included in the package are two pop-up characters and a paper doll. The contents in both the flat pack and the box version are the same. The costume in the box version was made in China. The costume in the flat pack was made in China. *Boxed fashion, courtesy of Mindy Jackson.*

Disney characters © Disney Enterprises, Inc.

Disney Classics Cinderella
Cinderella's Rags Dress
#1347 • 1992 • $35-45

Disney Classics "*Cinderella's* Rags Dress" was sold in two different package styles. The first releases were in a square box. *Cinderella* had lots of accessories. They included a one-piece brown cotton dress with long blue sleeves. Her apron is a woven linen-looking fabric with golden "pixie dust" with a triangle headscarf to match. She had a brown plastic pail, a bar of soap and a scrub brush for the floor. To serve her mean stepmother and stepsisters, she had a powder blue teapot, two cups and two saucers that she would carry on a matching serving tray. Included in this package are two pop-up characters. *Cinderella's* shoes are brown slip-on flats. The flat pack came with all the same accessories but with one less pop-up character. The fashion in this package was made in China.

Disney characters © Disney Enterprises, Inc.

CINDERELLA

Disney characters © Disney Enterprises, Inc.

Disney Classics Cinderella
Cinderella's Ballgown
#1275 • 1991 • $40-50

Disney Classics *Cinderella's Ballgown* came in either a box version or flat pack as did her Rags Dress. Her dress is made of pink and white satin with a nylon slip and a nylon flounce on her detachable floor-length skirt. The gown has removable collar, bows and skirt. *Cinderella's* accessories include a blue plastic necklace, pink satin hair ribbon and closed-toe pumps with molded bows. There are two pop-up characters. The box version was made in China. The flat pack was made in China.

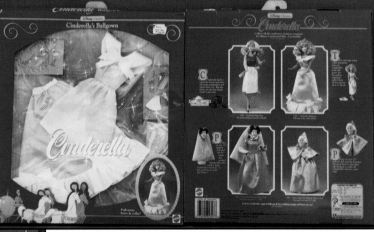

Disney characters © Disney Enterprises, Inc.

Disney Classics Cinderella
Cinderella Gift Pack • No stock
No date • $150-175

Disney Classics *Cinderella* Gift Pack has got to be one of the rarest Disney doll items you will ever come across. It is believed, but not confirmed, that this may well have been a display prop that Mattel made up and never distributed to shopkeepers. Three previously described items have been mounted on purple cardboard. It contains the standard Disney Classics *Cinderella* doll; *Cinderella's* "Rags Dress" and her "Ballgown." The value in this combination is due to the unique packaging. Although there is no origin of manufacturing, the three items that are mounted on the backboard in this photo were all made in China.

45

Disney characters © Disney Enterprises, Inc.

Disney characters © Disney Enterprises, Inc.

Disney Classics Cinderella
Cinderella Magical Bubble Ballroom
#2416 • 1991 • $145-155

Disney Classics *Cinderella* Magical Bubble Ballroom is one of my favorite display props. It comes with the Ballroom stage that requires adult assembly. There are two different changeable display backdrops. You get a special stand that has a mechanism built in so the dolls appear to dance. There is also a bubble blowing mechanism, a crown, a wand and instructions on assembly and use. Bubble solution was not included in this set. The stage in this photo was made in Italy.

Disney characters © Disney Enterprises, Inc.

Disney characters © Disney Enterprises, Inc.

CINDERELLA

Disney Classics Cinderella
Cinderella Wedding Carriage & Horse Set
#2422 • 1991 • $145-155

Disney Classics *Cinderella* Wedding Carriage & Horse Set is loads of fun to play with. Included in this marvelous set is the carriage, horse, six horse shoes, bridle, horse plume headpiece, golden girth, four pale green horse ribbons, a pink satin pillow with white lace trim, a hairbrush and instructions. The carriage and fabric accessories in this photo were made in China and the rest was made in Mexico.

Disney characters © Disney Enterprises, Inc.

Disney characters © Disney Enterprises, Inc.

Disney characters © Disney Enterprises, Inc.

Disney characters © Disney Enterprises, Inc.

Disney characters © Disney Enterprises, Inc.

Disney Classics Cinderella
Cinderella Horse
#1628 • 1991 • $70-80

Disney Classics *Cinderella* Horse has a platinum tail and mane and has emerald green eyes. The mane and tail on the horse that comes with the *Cinderella's* carriage is golden colored with blue eyes. Included in this package is a pink satin saddle with "pixie dust," six horse shoes, a gold-tone bridle, pink headpiece, golden girth, four satin ribbons, a hairbrush and instructions. The horse in this photo was made in Mexico.

47

CINDERELLA

Disney characters © Disney Enterprises, Inc.

Walt Disney's Cinderella
Special Sparkles Cinderella
#12988 • 1994 • $65-75

Special Sparkles Cinderella doll wears a one-piece dove blue glittered ballgown with a white peplum and white puff sleeves. The photo gives the impression that it has long sleeves, but they are actually gauntlets. *Cinderella* comes with a blue satin hair ribbon. Her jewelry includes a pair of silver-tone earrings with a matching ring and a black satin choker ribbon. She comes with her own special stand and matching shoes. The doll in this photo was made in China. *Courtesy of Carolyn Klemovec.*

Disney characters © Disney Enterprises, Inc.

Disney characters © Disney Enterprises, Inc.

Walt Disney's Cinderella
Sparkle Eyes Cinderella
#14789 • 1995 • $50-60

Sparkle Eyes Cinderella doll is virtually the same doll and fashion as *Special Sparkles Cinderella*. I keep looking for something different to share with you, but I just can't find anything unique to each doll. If you find something, let me know. The packaging however, is markedly different. The package change and the striking similarity in the names keeps me confused. Compare the photos and see for yourself. The doll in this photo was made in China. *Courtesy of Michelle Walker.*

Disney characters © Disney Enterprises, Inc.

Walt Disney's Cinderella
Sparkle Eyes Cinderella
Deluxe Gift Set
#15211 • 1995 • $75-100

Sparkle Eyes Cinderella doll was also available as a gift pack, which was mounted on cardboard like *Jasmine* and *Cinderella*, pages 7 and 45. It came with a small castle locket that housed a miniature *Cinderella* and *Prince Charming*. Unfortunately I do not have one to show you. *Photo not available.*

Disney characters © Disney Enterprises, Inc.

Walt Disney Cinderella
Wedding Cinderella
#14232 • 1995 • $120-130

Wedding Cinderella doll celebrated Walt Disney's *Cinderella*'s 45th Anniversary. Walt Disney first released this heart warming animated movie in 1950. Over the years the Disney Corporation has re-released this film five times. It has won three Academy Awards. This elusive *Wedding Cinderella* was the first "wedding" themed Disney heroine doll for Toys R Us. *Cinderella's* wedding gown is dramatically different than any of the other wedding gowns to date. Included in this remarkable book box is a *Cinderella* doll with extremely soft blue eyes and eyeshadow and golden hair with Lurex strands. The gown is brilliant white iridescent fabric with a built-in peplum. Her accessories include a veil with three satin rosettes and a bouquet with three pale blue satin rosettes, three white satin rosettes and one pink one. Her jewelry includes silver-tone ring, matching stud earrings with pearl-like drops and a double strand pearl-like necklace with a heart drop. Her shoes are clear plastic with glitter. The doll is wearing lace stockings and has a blue garter with white lace that are not listed with the contents. *Cinderella* has her own special labeled wedding stand. The doll in this photo was made in China.

Disney characters © Disney Enterprises, Inc.

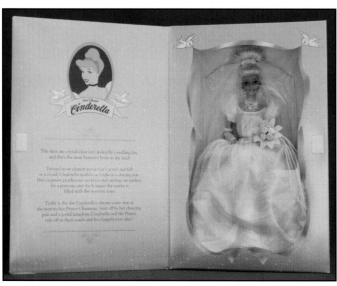

Disney characters © Disney Enterprises, Inc.

Disney characters © Disney Enterprises, Inc.

Walt Disney's Cinderella
Holiday Princess Cinderella
#16090 • 1996 • $120-130

Holiday Princess Cinderella doll was the first in a series of Disney Holiday dolls. She was classified as a Special Edition. Her white satin holiday ball gown is trimmed with faux fur on the peplum and around the neckline. The skirt is sprinkled with silver colored snowflakes which accent silver colored cardboard ornament, which was included in the box. There are four silver lamé bows on the gown, which match her hair ribbon. Her jewelry includes plastic silver earrings and matching ring and a white and silver lamé choker. Her shoes are clear closed-toe pumps with silver-tone glitter. The doll in this photo was made in China.

Disney characters © Disney Enterprises, Inc.

Disney characters © Disney Enterprises, Inc.

Disney characters © Disney Enterprises, Inc.

CINDERELLA

Walt Disney's Cinderella
Winter Dreams Cinderella
#18505 • 1997 • $60-70

Winter Dreams Cinderella doll was manufactured as a K B Toys Special Edition. She was the first in the Winter Dreams series for K B Toys. *Winter Dreams Cinderella* wears an ivory satin gown with lots of gold-tone trim ribbons and illusion-layered peplum and matching trimmed bubble sleeves. She has long white gloves, a hair ribbon and matching shoes. She comes with a pair of gold-tone stud earrings and a white and gold trim satin choker. Mattel re-cycled their Sear's customized *BARBIE®* doll "Ribbons and Roses" pattern for this gown. The doll in this photo was made in China.

Disney characters © Disney Enterprises, Inc.

Disney characters © Disney Enterprises, Inc.

Disney characters © Disney Enterprises, Inc.

CINDERELLA

Disney characters © Disney Enterprises, Inc.

Walt Disney's Cinderella
Signature Collection Cinderella
#19660 • 1998 • $75-85

Signature Collection Cinderella doll is the fourth in a series of collector dolls for Disney. This is the first Disney doll to have rooted eyelashes. Her scoop-neck ball gown is powder blue with short white chiffon sleeves with a matching peplum. The bodice is powder blue with silver Lurex thread and silver sequins, beads and rhinestones. The fabric of the skirt is remarkably like the fabric used on Mattel's very limited edition *Billions of Dreams BARBIE*® doll. Even the jewel decorations are the same. *Cinderella's* accessories include a pair of long white gloves; a blue satin hair ribbon and a pair of faux glass closed-toe platform shoes. Also included in her package are a signature stand, a pop-up and a certificate of authenticity. Her jewelry includes a pair of plastic silver-tone stud earrings with a matching ring and a black satin choker. The doll in this photo was made in Indonesia.

Disney characters © Disney Enterprises, Inc.

Disney characters © Disney Enterprises, Inc.

Walt Disney's Cinderella
Princess Stories Collection Cinderella
#18195 • 1997 • $20-30

Princess Stories Collection Cinderella doll wears a blue nylon floor length gown with iridescent long puff sleeves and peplum to match. The bodice has a delicate golden braid trim in the front. Included with this *Cinderella* doll, but not listed on the package is a pair of plastic pearl earrings, a blue satin hair ribbon, black choker and matching shoes. There is a Little Little Golden storybook and "Gus," a plastic mouse from the story. The *Little Little Cinderella* Golden Book was printed in the U.S.A. The doll in this photo was made in China.

Disney characters © Disney Enterprises, Inc.

Disney characters © Disney Enterprises, Inc.

CINDERELLA

Walt Disney's Cinderella
Disney Classics
Dress Up Dream™ Collection
#20419 • 1998 • $20-30

Dress-Up Dream Cinderella doll is wearing a powder blue nylon dress with short white puff netted sleeves with a peplum to match that is Chantilly lace trimmed. *Cinderella* has ten pastel satin bows, each with one satin streamer ribbon with faux pearl drops. The drops thread through the netting so you can dress-up your doll. Also included in the package is a white nylon sachet bag that matches her gauntlets. There is a blue satin ribbon in her hair and a black fabric choker. The only jewelry she wears is a pair of plastic pearl earrings. You also get a pearl colored plastic hairbrush and a clear pair of closed-toe pumps. The doll in this photo was made in China.

Disney characters © Disney Enterprises, Inc.

Disney characters © Disney Enterprises, Inc.

Walt Disney's Cinderella
Disney Classics
My Favorite Fairytale™ Collection
#21931 • 1998 • $18-22

My Favorite Fairytale Cinderella doll is one of three in the series. The other two are *Snow White* and *Alice* (See pages 107 and 146.) Each doll was assigned its own stock number. Stores could order the dolls by the assortment. The stock # for the assortment was #22039. *Cinderella* is wearing an all satin gown of two-tone blue. Her accessories include a hair ribbon, clear closed-toe pumps, and a pearl-colored hairbrush. *Cinderella's* jewelry includes a pair of white plastic earrings and black choker. The doll comes with mice, birds, pillow and slipper stand-up clip art. The doll in this photo was made in China.

Disney characters © Disney Enterprises, Inc.

Disney characters © Disney Enterprises, Inc.

55

HERCULES

Disney characters © Disney Enterprises, Inc.

Disney's Hercules
Golden Glow Hercules • #17112 • 1996 • $15-25

Golden Glow Hercules doll is very posable. He is jointed at the shoulders, elbows, knees and head. This action hero is a color change figure. When you put him in the sun his chest armor and overskirt change colors. Mattel does not recommend that you expose this toy to intense heat or direct sunlight for long lengths of time. The color change will automatically turn back to the original in about 1/2 hour. Hercules' chest armor and blue nylon cape and his bronze color overskirt are removable. He has a sienna color suede cloth headband and gold-tone wristbands, which match his armor and sword. He comes with nine decals. His shoes were specially designed just for him because he has extremely large feet that enable him to stand alone, but I do not advise shaking the table or he may fall over. The doll in this photo was made in China.

Disney characters © Disney Enterprises, Inc.   Disney characters © Disney Enterprises, Inc.

56

Disney characters © Disney Enterprises, Inc.

Disney's Hercules
Fashion Secrets Megara
#17149 • 1996 • $15-25

Disney's Fashion Secrets Megara, doll which is sometimes referred to as "Meg," has many changeable fashion looks. There are seven different ways shown on the back of her box. With the exception of her chiffon scarf, all the pieces are lavender and purple nylon. Her costume includes a dress, overskirt, shawl, sash, hair band and five clips. Included in the package are lace-up sandals and a hairbrush. There is also a smiling version not pictured. The doll in this photo was made in China.

Disney characters © Disney Enterprises, Inc.

Disney's Hercules
Fashion Secrets Megara Gift Set
#18044 • 1997 • $45-55

Disney's *Fashion Secrets Megara Gift Set* was available through the wholesale clubs and was mounted on cardboard. It came with a tiny locket that held a miniature *Hercules* and *Megara*. I unfortunately do not have one to show you. The doll and the fashion were the same as *Megara #17149*. *Photo not available.*

Disney characters © Disney Enterprises, Inc.

Disney characters © Disney Enterprises, Inc.

57

Disney characters © Disney Enterprises, Inc.

Disney's Hercules
Legend of Love Gift Set • #17479 • 1997 • $40-50

Legend of Love Hercules doll in this package is the same Hercules doll as Golden GlowHercules, but his ensemble is quite different. His top is a beautiful copper colored lamé with sky-blue shoulders that match his pleated satin skirt. Down his back is a deep teal blue nylon cape. His waist button, sword and wrist cuffs are from the same mold as on Golden Glow Hercules, but are tan rather than gold tone and his sandals are the same brown as with Golden Glow Hercules. The doll in this photo was made in China.

Legend of Love Megara doll's sleeveless v-neck gown is iridescent at the bodice and has an iridescent chiffon cape attached. The empire style dress is crystal pleated on the bottom and banded at the bust and waist with a golden braid. There is one flower with a faux pearl in the center on each shoulder. Meg has a wonderful toothy smile and unique Grecian golden drop earrings. This was the first and only "Meg" doll to have earrings. There was a second face mold available with a closed mouth. She wears gold tone plastic sandals that lace up her delicate ankles and calves. The doll in this photo was made in China.

Disney characters © Disney Enterprises, Inc.

Disney characters © Disney Enterprises, Inc.

Disney characters © Disney Enterprises, Inc.

Disney's Hercules
Megara Basic Doll
#17261 • 1997 • $12-17

Megara Basic Doll comes in a slim-line box. "Basic Dolls," as Mattel refers to them, are relatively fundamental and generally inexpensive. This Megara doll wears a simple turquoise nylon dress with golden braiding that crisscrosses her bustline and wraps around her waist. She has two golden buttons on her shoulders, which match her sandals. The doll in this photo was made in China.

Disney characters © Disney Enterprises, Inc.

HERCULES

Disney's Hercules Grecian Fantasy 'N Fun
#69268 • No box date
$10-14

"Grecian Fantasy 'N Fun" fashions for *Megara* doll shown here have the same stock numbers. The accessories shown on the back of the boxes are not what I found in the packages. Color substitutes are often made after the packaging has been developed. Arcotoys , Inc., a Mattel company, made both of these fashions in this photo in China.

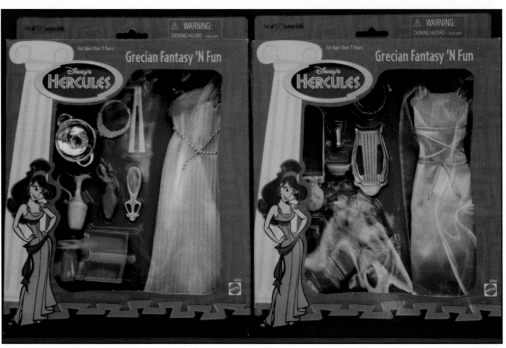

Disney characters © Disney Enterprises, Inc.

Disney characters © Disney Enterprises, Inc.

Disney characters © Disney Enterprises, Inc.

Disney's Hercules
Magic Wings Pegasus
#17254 • 1997 • $25-30

"Magic Wings Pegasus" is a battery operated horse. His wings actually flap as if he were flying. The resemblance of this horse to the one in the animated film is strikingly accurate. The wings were made in Mexico and the horse in this photo was made in China. *Courtesy of Michelle Walker.*

Disney's The Hunchback of Notre Dame Magic View Quasimodo
#15313 • 1995 • $20-30

Magic View Quasimodo doll is very rigid. He is referred to as "Magic View" because he comes with a "magic" lens that magnifies things. You can see it hanging around his neck. He is jointed at the shoulders and waist only. His outfit is olive green plastic. His legs are brown and his shoes are cadet blue. His brown work apron has pockets in which I have put his miniature ivory colored *Quasimodo, Esmeralda, Phoebus* and *Judge Claude Frollo*. One could also put his tools in the pockets. He comes with a brown molded plastic tool chest with a saw, mallet, paintbrush and knife. (Not shown.) The doll in this photo was made in China.

Disney characters © Disney Enterprises, Inc.

Disney characters © Disney Enterprises, Inc.

Disney characters © Disney Enterprises, Inc.

Disney's The Hunchback of Notre Dame
Esmeralda
#15311 • 1995 • $20-30

Esmeralda doll's face mold was a new one in 1995. The body style that Mattel used for this *Esmeralda* doll was the *Gymnast BARBIE®* body from 1994. This barefooted doll has larger feet than most Mattel dolls. She is jointed at the knee, elbows, shoulder, hip, waist and neck; this allows her to be very poseable. Although this package does not state that it is a gift set, it is considered one because it comes with an extra outfit. *Esmeralda* is holding her extra fashion on her arm. It is a round neck sleeveless nylon petticoat with turquoise satin ribbon lace up bodice, with a flounce at the hemline with three brass colored jingle bells. The costume that *Esmeralda* wears is a one-piece nylon dress with a built in suede-cloth cummerbund, which is trimmed in gold. The bodice is white and the skirt is lavender. Her detachable apron is grape colored with gold-tone stitching and seven plastic gold-tone gypsy bangles. Her headscarf is rose pink with golden glitter. Her jewelry includes four gold-tone bangle bracelets and one matching stud earring with a large hoop that is detachable. The doll in this photo was made in China.

Disney characters © Disney Enterprises, Inc.

Disney's The Hunchback of Notre Dame
Phoebus
#15312 • 1995 • $20-30

Phoebus doll has molded hair and beard. He is fully jointed at the neck, shoulders, elbows, waist and knees. His costume is rather elaborately constructed. His top is all one-piece bronze colored with built in sleeves, built in waistband belt and underneath a teal blue shirt which matches his detachable cape and pants. His gloves are suede cloth and are sewn separately. He has a silver and gold-tone sword in his belt. His pants are grape colored elastic pull-on at the top and boots are stitched to the nylon. The doll in this photo was made in China.

Disney characters © Disney Enterprises, Inc.

Disney's The Hunchback of Notre Dame
Gypsy Dancing Esmeralda
#15314 • 1995 • $ 25-35

Gypsy Dancing Esmeralda doll with her charcoal black hair has straight arms, jointed hips, a twist neck and waist. Her costume is elaborately glittered and the colors are vibrant and cheerful. Her dress is all one piece with two layers of orange chiffon over hot pink nylon. The top layer is bordered with gold lamé to match the trim around the scoop neck orange bodice. The sleeves and waist sash with two golden jingle bells are purple chiffon. The purple chiffon piece that you see over her shoulder with the gold sparkle sunburst is separate with a moon on the opposite side and two jingle bells on each end. The iridescent tassels you see falling from her wrist is a separate bracelet. In addition she has three separate golden plastic cuff bracelets. Her crown is hard golden plastic with an orange plastic jewel in the center. She has one golden plastic earring with large hoop to match. I am showing two boxes in the photo so that you can compare the foreign packaging to the American version. The special feature of this doll is that she comes with a musical tambourine. It works when attached to her wrist and a button when pushed, makes music and you can make her spin as if she is dancing. The batteries unfortunately are non-replaceable. The tambourine was made in China. The doll in this photo was made in Malaysia.

Disney characters © Disney Enterprises, Inc.

Disney's The Hunchback of Notre Dame True Hearts Gift Set
#15315 • 1996 • $40-50

True Hearts Gift Set has both *Esmeralda* and *Phoebus* dolls included. *Phoebus* wears the exact same outfit as the single doll does but his body is totally different. *Esmeralda's* gypsy costume is a one-piece nylon dress with a white long sleeve round necklace trim dress and a golden yellow sash. The skirt is jewel-tone purple; grape and teal green trimmed with green and gold color braiding. She wears a matching scarf in her hair with gold bangles. She has four gold-tone plastic bangle bracelets and one ankle bracelet and an earring to match. The only accessory she has is her non-musical tambourine with multi colored satin ribbons dangling from it and a grape colored hairbrush. Once again *Esmeralda* is barefooted. The dolls in this photo were made in China.

Disney's The Hunchback of Notre Dame
Gypsy Magic Horse
#15318 • 1995 • $ 20-30

"Gypsy Magic Horse" is solid white and has one of the most elegant manes and tail on any horse. It is platinum with gold Lurex threads. The "Gypsy Magic Horse" has blue eyes and gold lamé fabric reigns and saddle that are removable. Underneath the saddle is yellow, turquoise, purple and grape glittered chiffon. Below that is grape and royal blue nylon. By removing different layers you can make your horse look different. The horses costume was made in China, while the horse in this photo was made in Mexico. *Courtesy of Michelle Walker.*

Disney characters © Disney Enterprises, Inc.

Disney characters © Disney Enterprises, Inc.

Disney characters © Disney Enterprises, Inc.

Disney characters © Disney Enterprises, Inc.

Disney's The Hunchback of Notre Dame
Esmeralda Gypsy Festival Tent • #66234 • No date • $18-22

Esmeralda Gypsy Festival Tent is a fun prop to own. It comes with all the goodies that you see in the photo, however, colors can vary from one set to the other. This set was made by Arcotoys, Inc., which is a Mattel company. This set was made in China.

Disney characters © Disney Enterprises, Inc.

Disney's The Hunchback of Notre Dame
Esmeralda Deluxe Gift Set • #16204 • No date • $35-45

Esmeralda Deluxe Gift Set includes an *Esmeralda* doll, "Celestial Dream" fashion and "Festival of Fools" fashion. The package states that it was put together by Arcotoys, Inc., a Mattel Company. The fashions were made in China and the doll was made in either Malaysia or China.

THE HUNCHBACK OF NOTRE DAME

Disney's The Hunchback of Notre Dame
Magic Braids Esmeralda
#16001 • 1996 • $40-45

Magic Braids Esmeralda is a very large doll. Her dress is orange nylon with grape chiffon scarves that are embellished with golden glitter. They have jingle bells and the scarves can be removed to adorn her hair. She has several bangle bracelets and one hoop earring. There are ten hair braids with clips that can be added to her already beautiful black hair or golden headpiece. Included in the package is a large grape colored plastic styling hairbrush. The doll in this photo was made in China.

Disney characters © Disney Enterprises, Inc.

Disney characters © Disney Enterprises, Inc.

Disney's The Hunchback of Notre Dame
Dress 'n Play Festival of Fools
#66231 • No date • $4-8

Dress 'n Play Esmeralda's "Festival of Fools" fashion dress and accessories can be seen clearly. There may well have been variations. I did not make a mistake on the stock number; the same number was assigned to each item. I would presume that this is because they were sold as an assortment. These fashions were made by Arcotoys, Inc.; a Mattel company in China.

Disney characters © Disney Enterprises, Inc.

Disney's The Hunchback of Notre Dame
Dress 'n Play True Love
#66231 • No date • $4-8

Dress 'n Play Esmeralda's "True Love" large flat pack fashion dress and accessories can be seen clearly. There may well have been variations. These fashions were made by Arcotoys, Inc.; a Mattel company in China.

THE HUNCHBACK OF NOTRE DAME

Disney's The Hunchback of Notre Dame Fashion Assortment
#66230 • No date • $4-8

"Celestial Dream," "Dance Fantasy," "Dancing Pretty," "Festival of Fools" fashions.

     Esmeralda's small flat pack fashions included four different styles. However, I was able to find a variation on "Celestial Dream." It would not surprise me if you were to tell me that you have a variation of any of the others. Like "Dress 'n Play," all four styles have the same stock number and are probably the result of an assortment. These fashions were made by Arcotoys, Inc.; a Mattel company in China.

Disney characters © Disney Enterprises, Inc.

Disney characters © Disney Enterprises, Inc.

Disney's The Hunchback of Notre Dame Esmeralda Basic #16960 • 1996 • $18-22

Esmeralda Basic Doll is called "basic" because it is a "no-frills" doll. This is the type of doll that mothers should consider buying for small children. *Esmeralda* has straight arms and smooth plastic. This is a good doll for young children to play with because it is easy to dress and undress. This "basic" doll comes with a pink wraparound skirt, a swimsuit and a chiffon belt that can also be used as a hair tie. *Esmeralda* has a large single hoop earring. The doll in this photo was made in Malaysia. *Courtesy of Michelle Walker.*

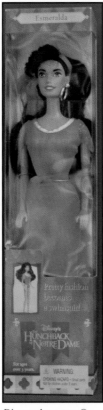

Disney characters ©
Disney Enterprises, Inc.

Disney characters © Disney Enterprises, Inc.

Disney characters © Disney Enterprises, Inc.

Disney's The Hunchback of Notre Dame
Phoebus, Quasimodo, Esmeralda, Hugo • No stock # • 1996 • $6-$8 each

The four dolls are made of plastic and cloth. Each of them has a label on them that states they were manufactured for Burger King Corporation ©Disney, Made in China. No where on the "dolls" does it say Mattel, yet a Mattel pamphlet is included in the plastic baggie that they were originally sold in. The dolls in this photo were made in China. *Courtesy of Meghann "Monkey" Walker.*

THE LITTLE MERMAID

Disney's The Little Mermaid
Basic Ariel
#17595 • 1997 • $14-18

The Little Mermaid Ariel doll is referred to by Mattel, as a "basic" doll. This term is not stated anywhere on the box. This is a relatively new term coined for slim-line box dolls that are inexpensive starter dolls for children to play with. There are few accessories included with "basic" dolls and have no small parts for young children to swallow. *Ariel* comes with a lavender bandeau swimsuit with matching bottoms and a peacock blue skirt with mint green fins. Tyco owned the rights to "Little Mermaid." When Mattel bought the company, they then got the license for "The Little Mermaid." So, prior to 1997 you will note that Tyco made *Ariel*. The doll in this photo was made in China.

Disney characters © Disney Enterprises, Inc.

Disney characters © Disney Enterprises, Inc.

71

THE LITTLE MERMAID

Disney characters © Disney Enterprises, Inc.

Disney's The Little Mermaid Princess Mermaid Ariel
#17593 • 1997 • $25-25

The Little Mermaid Princess Ariel doll is wearing a two piece mermaid outfit and comes with an extra princess dress. Her two piece mermaid outfit has an iridescent bandeau top with a nylon-printed bottom, which reverses to iridescent lavender to match her top. The fabric is custom printed with "Flounder" and "Sebastian." The "Princess" dress is a strapless gown trimmed with faux sea pearls and has detachable puff sleeves. The skirt is pale pink iridescent and glittered chiffon. She comes with a gold plastic crown and a matching starfish clip, fork and white pearl colored hairbrush. Included in the package but not listed is a pair of pale pink flats. The doll in this photo was made in China.

Disney characters © Disney Enterprises, Inc.

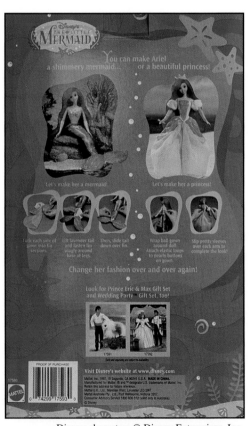

Disney characters © Disney Enterprises, Inc.

THE LITTLE MERMAID

Disney characters © Disney Enterprises, Inc.

Disney's The Little Mermaid Prince Eric & Max Gift Set
#17591 • 1997 • $22-25

The Little Mermaid *Prince Eric* and "Max" Gift Set is made special because of *Eric* doll's loyal companion, "Max" the sheepdog. He has long gray and white hair with a candy pink tongue. He is wearing a bandana that doubles as a cummerbund for *Eric*. *Eric* wears a white long sleeve shirt with dark blue pants. His knee-high boots are black and cadet blue faux leather. Included in this package is a red hairbrush for "Max." *Eric* doesn't need a brush since he has molded hair. The doll in this photo was made in China.

Disney characters © Disney Enterprises, Inc.

73

THE LITTLE MERMAID

Disney characters © Disney Enterprises, Inc.

Disney's The Little Mermaid
Aqua Fantasy Ariel
Film Premiere Edition
#17827 • 1997 • $80-90

The Little Mermaid Aqua Fantasy Ariel doll was a first, first, and first. It is the first in the "Film Premiere Edition" and it is the first collector *Ariel*. She was the first *Ariel* I took a fancy to. Her mermaid costume has a satin finish, deep sea green that is exceedingly form-fitting. It has only one delicate lace sleeve with faux seed pearls, which is the same as the lace that is swirl wrapped around her dress. Attached to the lace are three golden starfish and plastic crystals. *Ariel's* collar and fins are crystal pleated iridescent chiffon. Her accessories include a pair of white plastic pearl earrings and a matching shell doll stand with a clear waist clip. The book box is sea green and silver metallic with a window that is framed with a strip of film. It comes complete with a colorful *The Little Mermaid* scene. The doll in this photo was made in China.

Disney characters © Disney Enterprises, Inc.

Disney characters © Disney Enterprises, Inc.

THE LITTLE MERMAID

Disney's The Little Mermaid
Sea Witch Ursula
Great Villains Collection
Limited Edition
#17575 • 1997 • $95-115

The Little Mermaid Ursula doll is a Limited Edition. The suggested retail was more than many wanted to spend for such an unusual doll. They were not plentiful. Her packaging is so elaborate that I feel the box alone is worth the price. The multi purple box is a pop out door style. The background liner is iridescent purple, aqua, silver and blue bubbles. *Ursula* is made of lavender plastic and is only jointed at the shoulders. She is wearing a black velveteen strapless costume and her legs are a silk-look rich purple satin with sequins and beads to match. Her accessories include a golden shell necklace, scepter and crown and special decal *Ursula* doll stand. This doll is the third in the Great Villains Collection. The doll in this photo was made in China.

Disney characters © Disney Enterprises, Inc.

Disney characters © Disney Enterprises, Inc.

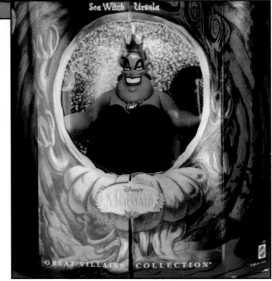

Disney characters © Disney Enterprises, Inc.

THE LITTLE MERMAID

Disney's The Little Mermaid
Tropical Splash Ariel
#17842 • 1997 • $14-18

The Little Mermaid Tropical Splash Ariel doll as with the entire *Tropical Splash* dolls, does not have legs. From their waists down to their fins the dolls are molded in hard plastic. This was a disappointment to some collectors, although children seemed to love it. *Ariel's* costume is blue and green. She comes with a flower and ribbon hair ornament. When dipped in warm water *Ariel's* costume changes from blue to lime green and printed flowers become more vibrant. Her lei, which can be worn as a child's bracelet, turns yellow in warm water. The doll in this photo was made in China.

Disney characters © Disney Enterprises, Inc.

Disney characters © Disney Enterprises, Inc.

Disney characters © Disney Enterprises, Inc.

Disney characters © Disney Enterprises, Inc.

Disney's The Little Mermaid
Tropical Splash Arista
#18696 • 1997 • $14-18

The Little Mermaid Tropical Splash Arista doll functions and comes with the same accessories as were described on the *Ariel* doll. *Arista's* costume is decorated with fish and the colors turn from cherry red to orange. The doll in this photo was made in China.

THE LITTLE MERMAID

Disney characters © Disney Enterprises, Inc.

Disney's The Little Mermaid
Tropical Splash Attina • #18694 • 1997 • $14-18

The Little Mermaid Tropical Splash Attina doll functions and comes with the same accessories as were described on the *Ariel* doll. *Attina's* costume is decorated with shells and starfish. The colors turn from purple to pink. The doll in this photo was made in China.

Disney's The Little Mermaid
Tropical Splash Kayla
#18695 • 1997 • $14-18

The Little Mermaid Tropical Splash Kayla doll functions and comes with the same accessories as were described on the *Ariel* doll. *Kayla's* costume is decorated with seahorses and the colors turn from orange to yellow. The doll in this photo was made in China.

Disney's The Little Mermaid
Tropical Splash Eric
#18478 • 1997 • $14-18

The Little Mermaid Tropical Splash Eric doll is the only one in the collection that comes with an extra plastic character that sucks in water and then spits it out. His navy blue, knee-length swim trunks have a print which appears when they are submerged in warm water. His lei is green, just like *Ariel's*. The doll in this photo was made in China.

Disney characters © Disney Enterprises, Inc.

Disney characters © Disney Enterprises, Inc.

Disney characters © Disney Enterprises, Inc.

Disney characters © Disney Enterprises, Inc.

THE LITTLE MERMAID

Disney's The Little Mermaid Valentine Ariel
#18459 • 1997 • $25-35

The Little Mermaid Valentine Ariel doll was a Target exclusive. She is hard to find. It seems they did not make very many of her. Her red hair is elbow length. She wears an aqua crown with an iridescent heart in the center, which matches her choker and cuff bracelet. There is also an iridescent raspberry and silver-tone heart with a raspberry ribbon. The bodice of her costume is feminine pink chiffon with red flocked hearts. The bandeau top is iridescent pink that matches her gauntlets and her fins. The skirt is a softer iridescent pink. Included in her package is a pale pink hairbrush. The doll in this photo was made in China.

Disney characters © Disney Enterprises, Inc.

Disney characters © Disney Enterprises, Inc.

Disney characters © Disney Enterprises, Inc.

Disney characters © Disney Enterprises, Inc.

Disney's The Little Mermaid
Swimming Ariel
#17562 • 1997 • $ 25-30

Swimming Ariel doll has a unique mechanism built in that allows her to actually swim with just a simple push of a button in her back. Her two piece mermaid costume changes colors when it is submerged in warm water. The ensemble will change back to the original when dipped in cold water or will return to original in a few minutes without assistance. Included in the package is a fish shaped hair comb. The doll in this photo was made in Malaysia.

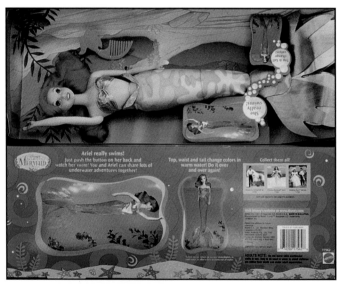

Disney characters © Disney Enterprises, Inc.

Disney characters © Disney Enterprises, Inc.

THE LITTLE MERMAID

Disney's
The Little Mermaid
Let's Swim Ariel
#18929 • 1997 • $30-40

The Little Mermaid 2-doll gift set is darling with *Merbaby Sandy* doll. She is wearing a mermaid costume to match *Ariel's* except hers is trimmed with pink and has a matching pink chiffon bonnet. *Ariel's* mermaid costume is bright yellow with a green, blue, red pink and orange fish print. Their fins are removable; both dolls have legs and both dolls' braids change color in warm water. Included in the package are an inflatable lavender star-shaped swim tube, a baby bottle, a star clip and a lavender hairbrush. The dolls in this photo were made in China.

Disney characters © Disney Enterprises, Inc.

Disney characters © Disney Enterprises, Inc.

Disney characters © Disney Enterprises, Inc.

THE LITTLE MERMAID

Disney characters © Disney Enterprises, Inc.

Disney's The Little Mermaid
Sea Pearl Princess Ariel
#18327 • 1997 • $25-35

The Little Mermaid Sea Pearl Princess Ariel doll was the first Avon Exclusive. Her box is the shoebox style that I like so much. *Ariel's* hair is knee length. Her swim top is iridescent purple and aqua to match the waistband on her fins and flippers. Her tapered skirt is a shiny peacock color. Around her wrist she carries a fuchsia colored net bag with a faux pearl and golden plastic shell charm bracelet for a child to wear. The doll in this photo was made in China.

Disney characters © Disney Enterprises, Inc.

81

THE LITTLE MERMAID

Disney characters © Disney Enterprises, Inc.

Disney's The Little Mermaid Ocean Bride Ariel
#18628 • 1997 • $30-35

The Little Mermaid Ocean Bride Ariel doll is wearing a marvelous two piece satin wedding gown with a layer of airy illusion that is heavily sprinkled with glitter that matches her veil. The bodice, peplum and overskirt are trimmed with orchid colored piping. *Ariel* has plastic pearl drop earrings and a wedding ring to match. Her wedding shoes are white closed-toe pumps. Her accessories include a three-tier wedding cake with a picture of the happy couple on top. There are also two presents made from lightweight cardboard. There are two pop-out doves, which appear to fly around her hair. The doll in this photo was made in China. *Courtesy of Michelle Walker.*

Disney characters © Disney Enterprises, Inc.

Disney characters © Disney Enterprises, Inc.

THE LITTLE MERMAID

Disney characters © Disney Enterprises, Inc.

Disney's The Little Mermaid
Wedding Party Gift Set • #17592 • 1997 • $32-38

The Little Mermaid Wedding Party Gift Set is a marvelous two doll gift set with "Flounder" and "Sebastian" carrying *Ariel* and *Eric's* wedding rings in a shell. First you get a beautiful *Ariel* doll bride wearing a white satin gown with puff sleeves and gauntlets. The bodice and petal peplum is trimmed with lavender satin stitching. The skirt is satin with a glittered illusion overskirt decorated with the same lavender trim as the bodice. She has a gold colored crown veil with glittered illusion to match her skirt. Listed with the contents is a molded pillow with rings, however there was not one included in my box. There was included but not listed, a pair of white plastic drop earrings and a white button wedding ring and a pair of white plastic pearl shoes.

    Eric is wearing a handsome wedding suit. His jacket is white satin and is adorned with cadet blue suede cloth collar and oversize cuffs with a detachable white satin ribbon banner. It is garnished with gold-tone suede cloth epaulettes, golden braiding and six imitation oval buttons. His pants are suede cloth to match his collar and cuffs and trimmed with the same golden braiding. His boots are faux black leather with red braiding to match *Ariel's* hair. Also included in this gift set is a white pearl-like hairbrush. The dolls in this photo were made in China.

Disney characters © Disney Enterprises, Inc.

Disney characters © Disney Enterprises, Inc.

Disney characters © Disney Enterprises, Inc.

Disney's The Little Mermaid
Picnic Party Gift Set • #18985 • 1997 • $50-60

The Little Mermaid Picnic Party Gift Set was an Exclusive Edition sold originally at Toys R Us. *Ariel* is wearing a nylon, aqua long sleeve dress with a lavender nylon and suedecloth strapless vest with golden criss-cross braiding. Her skirt is sea-blue nylon with an "A" pleat that is loaded with glitter. *Ariel* has a wide aqua satin ribbon in her waist length hair. Her jewelry is aqua plastic earrings and matching ring. She comes with aqua blue flats. *Eric's* shirt is almost identical to *Ariel's*; his shirt is aqua nylon with a vest just like *Ariel's*. His pants are textured steel gray. His boots are leatherette black and blue. There wouldn't be a picnic for the happy couple if it weren't for the picnic accessories, which include a white plastic hinged picnic basket, a yellow ice bucket, two yellow plates, knives, forks and spoons. In addition you get two champagne glasses with lavender floral napkins, and a champagne bottle. You also get a blue and yellow chipboard printed "blanket." There is a blue hairbrush for *Ariel*. The dolls in this photo were made in China.

Disney characters © Disney Enterprises, Inc.

Disney characters © Disney Enterprises, Inc.

Disney characters © Disney Enterprises, Inc.

Disney's The Little Mermaid
Dress 'N Play Fashions • #69291 • No box date • $10-15

The Little Mermaid Dress 'N Play fashions were made by Arcotoys, Inc., a Mattel company. Each of these ensembles came with an assortment of accessories that can be seen clearly in the boxes. ARCOTOYS, INC has written a message on the box, which states that the colors and decorations may vary. The fashions in this photo were made in China. *Courtesy of Michelle Walker.*

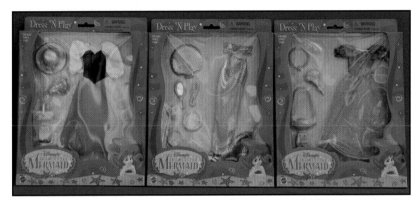

Disney characters © Disney Enterprises, Inc.

Disney characters © Disney Enterprises, Inc.

Disney's The Little Mermaid
Bedroom Set
#65928 • No box date • $25-30

The Little Mermaid Bedroom Set comes with a ton of goodies. The accessories are all pictured on the box. ARCOTOYS states on the box that colors and decorations may vary, that there is adult assembly required and the doll pictured is not included. The accessories include: a shell bed, vanity, chair, comb, necklace, headband, hand mirror, perfume bottle, bedside table, breakfast tray, photo frame, lamp, coffeepot, coffee cup, saucer and lamp stand. The bedroom set in this photo was made in China. *Courtesy of Michelle Walker.*

Disney characters © Disney Enterprises, Inc.

MULAN

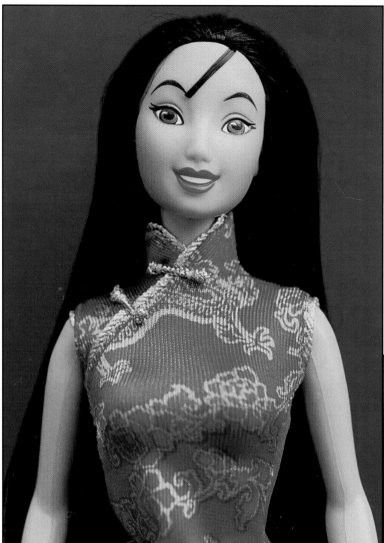

Disney characters © Disney Enterprises, Inc.

Basic Mulan doll is reported to have two different print dresses, both with scarlet and gold. I only have the one to show you. She is jointed at the neck, shoulders waist and knees. This allows wonderful display poses and permits her to ride her horse "Khan." Her hair is rich like black onyx. Listed on the back of the package is a scroll. I think of a scroll as paper that is rolled up like a poster, but in my doll it is a piece of printed chipboard that says, "Happiness is following your dreams." The doll in this photo was made in Indonesia.

Disney characters © Disney Enterprises, Inc.

MULAN

Disney characters © Disney Enterprises, Inc.

Disney's Mulan
Captain Li Shang
#18897 • 1997 • $18-24

Captain Li Shang doll is dressed in his warrior fashion. His jacket has dragons in circles, is trimmed with navy blue piping and is made to look like silk. He has a scarlet colored nylon waistband. His navy pants are simulated cotton and are stitched to his beige knit socks. His accessories include a golden and silver-tone sword and a warrior stick that when attached to his wrist allows him to perform martial art moves. There is a Yin-Yang bracelet for you to wear. Also, included in the package, but not listed, is a parchment colored scroll tied with a gold lamé ribbon. The doll in this photo was made in China.

Disney characters © Disney Enterprises, Inc.

Disney characters © Disney Enterprises, Inc.

MULAN

Disney characters © Disney Enterprises, Inc.

Disney's Mulan
Secret Hero Mulan • #18896 • 1997 • $20-28

Secret Hero Mulan doll had me nervous when I read the inside mini poster that says "Cut" her hair; I thought Mattel was encouraging little children to cut their dolls hair. I was very relieved when I discovered that her ponytail is in fact detachable! *Mulan's* jacket is purple satin with red trim with a satin ribbon belt. Her pants are purple elastic pull-on with lavender nylon from the knee down. She comes with an extra red, gold, black and purple wrap around skirt. Her accessories include a silver and gold colored plastic sword, a spin stick, a parchment scroll with a golden ribbon tie, and black molded flats. It is interesting to compare the fronts of the two packages because *Mulan* was positioned two different ways. The dolls in this photo were made in China.

Disney characters © Disney Enterprises, Inc.

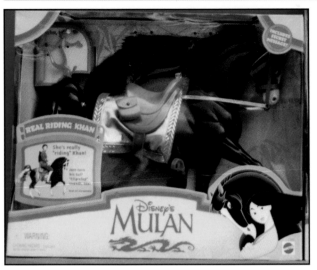

Disney characters © Disney Enterprises, Inc.

Disney characters © Disney
Enterprises, Inc.

Disney's Mulan
Real Riding Khan • #19095 • 1997 • $25-35

"Real Riding Khan" horse had all the same amenities as "Real Riding Khan" Gift Set, except there was no *Mulan* doll included in the box. For further detail see the information on "Real Riding Khan" Gift Set.

Disney characters © Disney Enterprises, Inc.

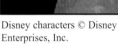

Disney characters © Disney Enterprises, Inc.

Disney characters © Disney
Enterprises, Inc.

Disney's Mulan
Real Riding Khan Gift Set • #18994 • 1997 • $50-60

"Real Riding Khan" is *Mulan's* trusty companion. This black horse with four white feet is designed to make "clip-clop" sounds by simply putting *Mulan's* feet in the stirrups, turn his tail from side to side and off she "rides." He comes with a purple plastic saddle, a lovely purple lamé saddle blanket that is trimmed in red and gold fabric. His bridle is purple and his reigns are golden ribbon. There is an extra red satin ribbon to dress his tail. There is a teal green plastic saddlebag. *Mulan's* fashion is a two piece pantsuit. The jacket is red brocade trimmed with gold lamé down the front and at the cuffs. There is matching gold lamé from her knees down. She wears red plastic molded flat shoes. Included in this wonderful gift set is a plastic "Mushu" character and a paper scroll with a lamé ribbon tied around it. "Khan" and *Mulan* in this gift set were made in China.

Disney characters © Disney Enterprises, Inc.

MULAN

Disney characters © Disney Enterprises, Inc.

Disney's Mulan
Hearts of Honor Gift Set
#19019 • 1997 • $45-55

Hearts of Honor Gift Set features *Mulan* and *Shang dolls* in enchanting pistachio green coordinating fashions. *Mulan's* gown has lavender long sleeves to match the bodice of her dress, which is trimmed with floral banding. There is a rich copper colored lamé sash with a golden braid tie. The skirt is pistachio colored and has pale blue floral print on it. She has a lavender chiffon floor-length shawl. Her other accessories include a flower in her hair, a purple hair comb, jade colored drop earrings, and lavender flat shoes.

Shang's costume wraps around at his waist. He carries his sword in this attached waistband. There is a golden ribbon in his rooted hair. His legs are an unusual pale green color. (No, I cannot explain this.) He has flat black slip on shoes. There is also an orange scroll included in this gift set that is tied with a golden color ribbon. The dolls in this photo were made in China.

Disney characters © Disney Enterprises, Inc.

Disney characters © Disney Enterprises, Inc.

MULAN

Disney's Mulan
Matchmaker Magic Mulan • #18991 • 1997 • $25-35

Matchmaker Magic Mulan doll has lots of versatility. Her fashion is reversible and comes with innumerable accessories so she can have many different looks. Mattel suggests dipping her powder puff in warm water and applying it to her face to have it change from flesh-tone to white. If you do this, be careful not to drip on her satin dress or it will cause watermarks on the fabric. Her face will change to white in the sun in just a few seconds, so this is an alternative for you.

She wears a one-piece dress; pink satin at the top, trimmed with purple crisscross banding with a turquoise chiffon scarf stitched to the inside of the neckline and she has large turn-up cuffs of white satin. The floor length skirt is also white satin to match the cuffs. The lavender panel with pink leaf print, from the bodice, reverses to solid lavender and has a Yin and Yang. The scarlet satin underskirt that you see with brilliant golden flowers reverses to solid garnet. You can easily transform *Mulan* from a village girl into a princess.

Mattel continually amazes me with new concepts in hair styling. *Mulan* comes with a pull-tab in the center of her back. When you pull the cord out her hair instantly bunches up into a bun. She comes with three separate purple hair twists so you can decorate her ponytail when it is down. *Mulan* wears a pair of plastic jade colored button earrings and a bead choker to match. Other accessories included in this package are a powder bowl, powder puff, two hair combs, a pink scroll with golden ribbon, a put-together parasol, instructions and a pair of grape colored flat shoes. The doll in this photo was made in China.

MULAN

Disney characters © Disney Enterprises, Inc.

Disney characters © Disney Enterprises, Inc.

Disney's Mulan
Imperial Beauty Mulan
Film Premiere Edition
#18991 • 1998 • $70-80

Disney's *Imperial Beauty Mulan* doll is the second in the Film Premiere Edition Series. *Aqua Fantasy Ariel* precedes her. (See page 74.) *Mulan's* elegant gown is made from satin and gold lamé fabric with a sewn in white chiffon scarf. She wears a long sleeved regal garnet dragon print overlay that is trimmed with black and gold satin. The underskirt is chiffon and additional lamé fabric. The chiffon scarf with disks and tassels is not attached. The crown that adorns her head is quite elaborate; complete with a bird, a dragon and red beaded tassels. At the back of her hair are two dragon-headed hairpins. Hidden under her skirt and feet is a pair of red satin slippers. Her box has a wonderful cello window so you can see her without opening her book box. Be careful when opening this type of box because the Velcro™ closure if not handled properly can cause you to dent the box. Once you open the box a marvelous pop-out appears showing *Mulan* putting on her makeup. The entire doll and package is simple and elegant. Mattel's Disney Division's fabulous designer, Lisa Temming, designed *Imperial Beauty Mulan*. The doll in this photo was made in China.

Disney characters © Disney Enterprises, Inc.

92

Disney characters © Disney Enterprises, Inc.

MULAN

Disney's Mulan
Satiny Shimmer Mulan
#19432 • 1998 • $30-35

Satiny Shimmer Mulan doll was an Avon exclusive. She is the second gift box doll done for Avon. The first was *Sea Pearl Ariel*, see page 81. Her dress is a one-piece oriental floor length gown. It is very simple and tastefully done. The pastel pink bodice, white jade and gold-tone bodice and soft aqua dress match her makeup perfectly. *Mulan's* accessories include a fan; a pale pink scroll tied with a gold-tone ribbon and a matching hair comb. *Mulan* has flat feet, so consequently her shoes are flat. They are a deep blue-jade color. The doll in this photo was made in Indonesia. *Courtesy of Michelle Walker.*

Disney characters © Disney Enterprises, Inc.

Disney characters © Disney Enterprises, Inc.

Disney characters © Disney Enterprises, Inc.

Disney's Mulan
Mulan's Palace Playset • #67937 • no year on box • $20-25

The *Mulan Palace Playset* states that there is adult assembly required and that the doll shown on the box is not included. "Chirpin' Cri-kee," stock #82631 and "Talking Mushu," stock #69987 as seen on the box are not included either. The items contained in this box are: 2 Chinese tables, bowl with 3 perfume bottles, teapot with 2 cups, "Cri-kee" with cage, folding screen, fabric pillow, cookie box, mirror, and a hairbrush. This playset was made by ARCOTOYS, INC, a Mattel company. The playset in this photo was made in China. *Courtesy of Michelle Walker.*

Disney characters © Disney Enterprises, Inc.

Disney's Mulan
Far East Fashions • #67931 • No Date • $5-8

These "Far East Fashions" were made by Arcotoys, Inc., a Mattel company in China. There are three fashions in the collection, all of that have the same stock number as they were sold in an assortment. When you dress your Mulan dolls in these fashions and add them to your display, you will find it to be one of the most cheerful exhibitions you own.

Disney characters © Disney Enterprises, Inc.

OTHER FAMOUS CHARACTER DOLLS

Walt Disney's Pirates of the Caribbean
Captain
Disney Exclusive
#10258 • 1993 • $70-80

Pirates of the Caribbean Captain doll is exceptional. This is the first doll that Mattel made with a black rooted beard. Under all that facial hair is the face mold used for the *Prince* from *Beauty and the Beast*. His jacket is bright red with golden yellow pirate cuffs and "Pirates of the Caribbean Disney" embossed in gold-tone lettering. It is cinched at the waist with a brown suede cloth belt with built in sword holder. He has a matching shoulder strap, 3-dagger holder. (Silver-tone dagger seen on package.) *Captain's* pants are black cotton with knee high pirate boots, which match the trim on his jacket. His pirate hat is made out of black suede cloth, complete with skull and crossbones. Underneath his hat is a red nylon scarf that is hard to see in the photo. The face paint on this doll is absolutely unprecedented. Notice how precise his teeth are. The doll in this photo was made in China.

Disney characters
© Disney
Enterprises, Inc.

Walt Disney's Peter Pan de Walt Disney
Flying Peter Pan, #1
Disney Exclusive
#10719 • 1993 • $45-55

Flying Peter Pan doll has been issued two times. The first set of *Peter Pan* characters was originally done for Disney Stores, Theme Parks and was available in foreign markets only. 1993 marked the 40th anniversary of Walt Disney's *Peter Pan* animated film The second versions were exclusive to Disney and Toys R Us. There is no major difference between the first *Peter Pan* doll and the second one; both are 11-1/2 inches. The boxes however are considerably distinct. The first issues were written in multi languages. *Peter*'s costume has ragged short sleeve shirt which fits nicely over his olive green rib-knit pants. It is cinched at the waist with a brown belt with a knife holder. His silver colored knife is designed to wrap around his hand as if he was holding it. His boots are buff colored slip on moccasins. His hat and feather are molded into his head. Both *Peter Pan* dolls come with six feet of fish-line type wire so that one can simulate flying. The doll in this photo was made in China.

Disney characters © Disney Enterprises, Inc.

Disney characters © Disney
Enterprises, Inc.

Walt Disney's Peter Pan de Walt Disney
Flying Peter Pan, #2
#19296 • 1997 • $30-40

The major difference between the first and second *Peter Pan* doll is the packaging. The second releases are written in English only. The orange hair on the second version is one shade lighter, while his lips are considerably darker. Either one of these *Peter Pan's* are a delight to have in your collection. The doll in this photo was made in China.

Disney characters © Disney Enterprises, Inc.

Disney characters ©
Disney Enterprises, Inc.

Disney characters © Disney Enterprises, Inc.

Walt Disney's Peter Pan de Walt Disney
Flying Wendy, #1
Disney Exclusive
#10720 • 1993 • $45-55

Flying Wendy #1 doll's face mold was first used on Mattel's big-eyed *Teen Sweetheart Skipper* doll in 1988. Both *Wendy* #1 and *Wendy* #2 are 10 inches tall. *Wendy* has red hair with bangs. Her dress is blue nylon with a layer of chiffon with "pixie dust." There is a lavender ribbon in her hair and at her waist. Her shoes are teal blue flats. She comes with the same flying apparatus as with the *Peter Pan* dolls. The doll in this photo was made in Malaysia.

Disney characters © Disney Enterprises, Inc.

Walt Disney's Peter Pan
de Walt Disney
Flying Wendy, #2
#19297 • 1997 • $25-35

Wendy #2, doll four years after the first release experienced a face mold change. The face mold used on the second edition is the 1995 *Pizza Hut Courtney*. *Wendy* #2's costume is virtually the same as the first *Wendy's* dress. This *Wendy* has two little hair twists on her forehead instead of bangs. The doll in this photo was made in China.

Disney characters © Disney Enterprises, Inc.

Disney characters © Disney Enterprises, Inc.

Disney characters © Disney Enterprises, Inc.

OTHER FAMOUS CHARACTER DOLLS

Disney characters © Disney Enterprises, Inc.

Walt Disney's Peter Pan de Walt Disney
Flying Tinker Bell, #1
Disney Exclusive
#11762 • 1993 • $55-65

Flying Tinker Bell #1 doll has the *Homecoming Queen Skipper* face mold from 1987. She is a mere 10 inches tall. Her costume is constructed in two pieces. The strapless bodice is lime green glitter fabric overlaid with chartreuse plastic. The first layer of her skirt is also plastic with glittered chiffon below. Her elastic pull-on panties are shamrock green which match her slippers that have white pompons. *Tinker Bell's* wings are made from hard plastic, and are the most wonderful aspect of this doll. Her other accessories include a black satin hair ribbon, a wand, and a special hair clip to help her fly on her six-foot line. The doll in this photo was made in Malaysia.

Disney characters © Disney Enterprises, Inc.

Walt Disney's Peter Pan
de Walt Disney
Flying Tinker Bell, #2
#19298 • 1997 • $30-40

Flying Tinker Bell #2 doll has an extremely different hair do. The hair on this issue is lemon blonde and her make-up is amazingly different. Her costume is virtually the same with the exception of the wings, which are very plain. Compare the photos for visual detail. She comes with all the same accessories as the first version. The doll in this photo was made in China.

Disney characters © Disney Enterprises, Inc.

Disney characters © Disney
Enterprises, Inc.

**Walt Disney's
Masters of Malice
Captain Hook
#20954 • 1998 • $75-88**
Photo courtesy of Mattel.

Peter Pan
Tinker Bell Prototype

Mattel originally had in mind to make *Tinker Bell* for the motion picture film, *Hook*. The doll was to have been in the likeness of Julia Roberts who starred in the movie. For the prototype Mattel used the *Steffie* face mold. A stock number was assigned and this photo was distributed to some dealers to order from. Some photos got out into the market place, but unfortunately, this doll was never released. This doll was never manufactured. *Photo courtesy of Mattel.*

OTHER FAMOUS CHARACTER DOLLS

Disney characters © Disney Enterprises, Inc.

Disney's Bedtime Princess Collection
#A13726 • 1995 • Not Produced

Disney's Bedtime Princess Collection was a wonderful concept for younger children. These dolls had soft bodies and were huggable. Their gowns were made from silky like fabric that had the "glow-in-the-dark feature. Each doll plays a melody from the feature film. *Jasmine* plays "A Whole New World, *Belle* plays the melody from Beauty and the Beast, *Cinderella* plays "A Dream is a Wish," *Snow White* plays "Some Day My Prince Will Come" and *Sleeping Beauty* plays "Once Upon a Dream." Unfortunately these dolls were never released into the market place, although they were shown in the Mattel catalog. *Photo courtesy of Mattel.*

Disney's Aladdin
Disney's Bedtime Princess Collection
Jasmine • #A13726 • 1995

Disney's Beauty and the Beast
Disney's Bedtime Princess Collection
Belle • #A13726 • 1995

Walt Disney's Cinderella
Disney's Bedtime Princess Collection
Cinderella • #A13726 • 1995

Walt Disney's Sleeping Beauty
Disney's Bedtime Princess Collection
Sleeping Beauty • #A13726 • 1995

Walt Disney's Snow White
Disney's Bedtime Princess Collection
Snow White • #A13726 • 1995

Disney characters © Disney Enterprises, Inc.

Walt Disney's Davy Crockett
Davy Crockett
Disney Exclusive
#10308 • 1993 • $70-80

Davy Crockett doll's face mold is that of *Grandpa Heart* which was first introduced by Mattel back in 1987. He wears a faux buckskin two piece fringe-trimmed suit. He has a brown bag and belt made out of the same suede cloth as his American Indian influenced pantsuit. Naturally *Davy* doll would be wearing his faux fur coonskin cap complete with a faux raccoon tail. He has a knife, a knife sheath and a hatchet. His shoes are moccasin-like two-tone slip-ons. The doll in this photo was made in Malaysia. This doll was a Disney Park and a Disney catalog exclusive!

Disney characters © Disney Enterprises, Inc.

Disney characters © Disney Enterprises, Inc.

Walt Disney's Mary Poppins
Mary Poppins
Disney Exclusive
#10313 • 1993 • $80-90

Mary Poppins doll's face mold was not Julie Andrew's face; it is *Sleeping Beauty* doll's mold. Her costume is considerably more elaborate than it appears at first glance. Her red nanny skirt reverses to white chiffon for her "Jolly Holiday" fashion. Underneath her skirt she wears white nylon pantaloons. Her coat is navy blue with a large collar. The blouse is white nylon with a white chiffon ruffle topped with a red satin bow to match the bottom part of her blouse. *Mary Poppins* doll's accessories include a black two-piece umbrella that snaps together. She comes with two hats, a printed carpetbag, a red fringed scarf, a hairbrush and red molded lace-up boots. Included with my doll, but not listed on the package is a white plastic button ring. The doll in this photo was made in Malaysia.

Disney characters © Disney Enterprises, Inc.

OTHER FAMOUS CHARACTER DOLLS

Walt Disney's Alice in Wonderland
Alice in Wonderland
Disney Exclusive
#13537 • 1994 • $40-50

Alice in Wonderland doll was made from the 1978 copyright *Skipper* head mold. *Alice* wears a blue satin short-sleeve dress with "pixie dust" and lace trim at the hemline. Over her dress she wears a white cotton apron. She has white nylon stockings, a black satin hair ribbon and black flat shoes. Included in the box are two pop-out cardboard characters and a blue hairbrush. The doll in this photo was made in Malaysia.

OTHER FAMOUS CHARACTER DOLLS

Walt Disney's Alice in Wonderland
Disney Classics
My Favorite Fairytale™ Collection
#21933 • 1998 • $18-22

Disney Classics *My Favorite Fairytale Alice in Wonderland* doll is one of three in the series. The other two are Cinderella and Snow White. (See pages 55 and 146.) Each doll was assigned its own stock number. Stores could order the dolls by the assortment. The stock # for the assortment was #22039. Alice is wearing an all-satin blue dress with a white satin pinafore. Her accessories include a black satin hair ribbon, black plastic flats, a blue colored hairbrush. The doll comes with a "White Rabbit," "Cheshire Cat," "Dinah" and the "Dormouse" stand-up clip art. The doll in this photo was made in China.

Disney characters © Disney Enterprises, Inc.

Disney characters © Disney Enterprises, Inc.

OTHER FAMOUS CHARACTER DOLLS

Disney's 101 Dalmatians
Cruella De Vil - Power in Pinstripes
Great Villains Collection
#16295 • 1996 • $75-85

Cruella De Vil's likeness to Glenn Close is uncanny. She is from the "Great Villains Collection" and is the first in the series of Great Villains. The construction, the quality of workmanship, the attention to detail and the unique packaging make this one of the best values of 1996.

Her one-piece dress has a black nylon bodice with a wrap around pinstripe straight skirt. The jacket is also pinstripe with white glittered satin one-sided collar with white satin trim to match at the wrist. The jacket is adorned with two faux ivory teeth pins that have pewter colored trim. The simulated sable stole is wonderfully elegant with two white stripes and eight tails. The muff on her opposite arm has three white stripes; it is lined with white felt and has fringe draping to the floor. Cruella carries red sunglasses and wears a pair of black nylon gloves. She is holding a red cigarette holder in her right hand with a white cigarette at the end. Her pitch-black hat could be (James) Galanos or Lilly Daché inspired. It is the most dramatic piece in her costume. The crown of her hat is appropriately glittered, the band is stiff linen-like fabric and it has a Swiss dot netted veil. Her hair falls to her chin and is white on the left side and black on the right. The shoes are simple black closed-toe heels, which appear to be lace-ups, but are not.

The doll comes with her own special decal stand stating that she is *Cruella De Vil* and that she is a Collector Edition. The packaging with the pop out Greyhounds and mirror-back liner is extremely elegant against the pewter color front that is Art Deco in style. *Cruella De Vil Power in Pinstripes* should not be confused with *Power in Pinstripes BARBIE®* doll. The doll in this photo was made in China.

Disney characters © Disney Enterprises, Inc.

Disney characters © Disney Enterprises, Inc.

Disney characters © Disney Enterprises, Inc.

Disney characters © Disney Enterprises, Inc.

Disney's 101 Dalmatians
Cruella De Vil - Ruthless in Red
Great Villains Collection
#17576 • 1997 • $125-150

Cruella De Vil, Ruthless in Red doll's production level was considerably lower than *Cruella De Vil, Power in Pinstripes*. As a result of lower supply, the price difference is justifiable. Again, the resemblance to Glenn Close is remarkable and I just cannot say enough good things about these Disney dolls. *Ruthless in Red* wears a red turtle neck sweater over red vinyl leggings. The faux fur car coat is extraordinarily thick. She wears a red faux fur pillbox hat that allows you to see more of her hair. This doll's hair seems a tad shorter. It is befitting that *Cruella* is dressed in a car coat since her pop-out box has her sleek vintage two-door car. The packaging has the same pewter colored front as *Power in Pinstripes*. She comes with her own special decal stand. The doll in this photo was made in China.

Disney characters © Disney Enterprises, Inc.

OTHER FAMOUS CHARACTER DOLLS

Disney characters © Disney Enterprises, Inc.

Disney's Toy Story
Buzz Light Year To the Rescue
Special Edition Holiday Hero
Disney Holiday Collection
#19889 • 1998 • $50-55

Holiday Hero Buzz Light Year from *Toy Story* is really a fun action figure. His red, green silver and white metallic body is exactly how you would imagine him being. Notice the mistletoe over his head on the front of the box and you will find a sprig of plastic mistletoe inside the box as well. Which of you will be the first to kiss him? He has a retractable helmet that lights up. *Buzz* has a set of wings on the back of his suit that expands at the push of a button. There is even a button on his arm that allows him to make laser sounds. He has three buttons on his chest. When you push them he says four different phrases: "I wish you a happy Christmas and a happy light year." "To the North Pole and beyond." "This is Buzz Light Year, come in "Rudolf." "I protect Christmas presents from the threat of invasion." The doll in this photo was made in, no, not Toy Land, it was made in China.

Disney characters © Disney Enterprises, Inc.

Disney characters © Disney Enterprises, Inc.

ANNOUNCING...

Disney's Tarzan

At the time of the writing of this book, Mattel, Inc. had announced that they would be making several new famous character dolls for the 1999 release of *Disney's Tarzan* animated movie. Announced were: *Disney's Tarzan Jane Fashion Doll* #22345; *Disney's Tarzan and Jane Gift Set* #22188, and *Disney's Tarzan Ultimate Tarzan* #22446. The manufacturing country was not available at the time of this printing. Watch for Volume II to see the actual production dolls.

POCAHONTAS

Disney's Pocahontas
Sun Colors Pocahontas
#13328 • 1995 • $20-30

Sun Colors Pocahontas dolls are lots of fun because their outfits change colors when they are set in the sun. When placed in the sunlight *Pocahontas'* dress turns from solid beige to a leaf print. The first *Sun Colors Pocahontas* dolls that were released into the marketplace were supposed to include a child's "Flit" flutter ring. For some unknown reason the rings were not made in time to include in the package, so, Mattel made arrangements for buyers to send in a form and would later send the rings in the mail. When the rings were manufactured, Mattel went back to their original plan and mounted them on the liners. Early releases of the Sun Color dolls were in shades of purple and were later changed to shades of blue. (See below.) *Pocahontas* wears a one shoulder beige dress with copper and beige fringe at the neckline and hemline to match her belt. Around her wrist she has a compass and around her neck she has a turquoise plastic necklace with a simulated white tooth. She has a faux doeskin blanket with gold-tone- printed animals, acorns, trees, leaves, "Flit" and more. The barefooted doll in this photo was made in China.

Disney characters © Disney Enterprises, Inc.

Disney characters © Disney Enterprises, Inc.

Disney characters © Disney Enterprises, Inc.

Disney characters © Disney Enterprises, Inc.

Disney's Pocahontas
Sun Colors John Smith
#13329 • 1995 • $20-30

Sun Colors John Smith doll with his rooted hair and square jaw make him appear to be a very strong character. His shirt has powder blue epaulets and is beige suede cloth like *Pocahontas'* dress, but it does not change color. His pants are sky blue suede-cloth, elastic pull-ons. His accessories include a brown suede cloth bag with a black shoulder strap with sword holder and silver colored plastic sword. He wears a pewter colored vest and helmet. He comes with a compass locket with a picture of himself and *Pocahontas*. His boots are blue suede cloth moccasin style. The doll in this photo was made in China.

Disney characters © Disney Enterprises, Inc.

POCAHONTAS

Disney's Pocahontas
Sun Colors Nakoma
#13331 • 1995 • $20-30

Pocahontas Sun Colors Nakoma doll's two piece dress is solid two-tone bone colored that turns to a printed butterfly pattern when it is put in the sun. Her accessories include a brown and gray plastic fire pit and terra-cotta colored plastic pot. She has a faux doe skin blue colored blanket with the same gold-tone print as on *Pocahontas*'. The doll in this photo was made in China.

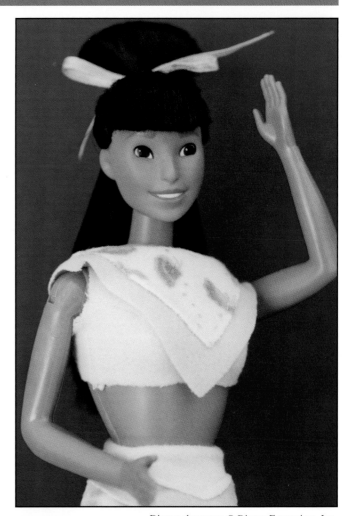

Disney characters © Disney Enterprises, Inc.

Disney characters © Disney Enterprises, Inc.

Disney characters © Disney Enterprises, Inc.

114

Pocahontas

Disney's Pocahontas
Sun Colors Kocoum
#13330 • 1995 • $20-30

Pocahontas Sun Colors Kocoum doll is the second male American
Indian that Mattel has made. The first was 10-inch *Nakoma* from the
TV show *Grizzly Adams* in 1978. He is fabulous to display with the
American Indian *BARBIE*® dolls from the Dolls of the World Series
as well as with the *Pocahontas* series. *Kocoum* has a long loincloth
that changes colors in the sun. The suede cloth fabric turns from tan
to American Indian symbols. He has copper colored cuffs to match
his belt of leatherette that is back lined with turquoise felt. He also
has a copper colored choker. He carries a traditional-look bow and
arrows in a holder with brown leatherette strap. The doll in this photo
was made in China.

Disney characters © Disney
Enterprises, Inc.

Disney characters © Disney Enterprises, Inc.

Disney characters © Disney Enterprises, Inc.

115

POCAHONTAS

Disney's Pocahontas
River Rowing Pocahontas
#13333 • 1995 • $35-45

Pocahontas River Rowing Pocahontas doll and canoe was not an inexpensive item, but it sure was a good value. Her canoe is motorized and the oars really do paddle. Of course, you need batteries, which had to be purchased separately. The motor, rudder and paddle are removable. Included in this gift set are a plastic "Meeko," a purple hairbrush and instructions. *Pocahontas'* two piece costume is pale peach with pale blue-green trees with brown trunks. The necklace she is wearing was used on quite a few of the different *Pocahontas* dolls. If you haven't noticed yet, all of *Pocahontas's* friends and accessories relate to the earth and the sun, as is the way of life for the American Indian. The doll in this photo was made in China.

Disney characters © Disney Enterprises, Inc.

Disney characters © Disney Enterprises, Inc.

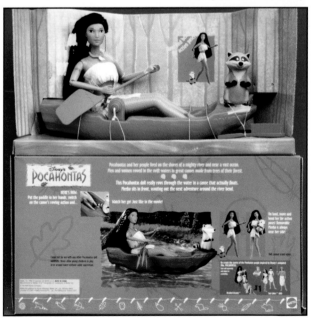

Disney characters © Disney Enterprises, Inc.

Disney characters © Disney Enterprises, Inc.

Disney's Pocahontas
Braided Beauty Pocahontas
#13332 • 1995 • $30-40

Pocahontas Braided Beauty Gift Set was not billed as a gift set, but you can see that it is because of the wonderful "Meeko" hair braider. Mattel first introduced the hair braid mechanism in 1982 with a doll called *Twirly Curls BARBIE*® doll. If you are so inclined you can make a lot of hairstyles for your doll with the braider and many hair clips and ribbons that are included in this package. *Pocahontas* wears a one shoulder dress which is the exact same pattern as was used for *Sun Colors Pocahontas*, only this one is made from apricot colored suede cloth fabric with bone colored fringe. The belt is copper and white and she has the same necklace as you have seen on the previous dolls. She comes with a purple hairbrush. The doll in this photo was made in China.

Disney characters © Disney Enterprises, Inc.

117

Disney's Pocahontas
Shining Braids Pocahontas
#15416 • 1995 • $20-30

Shining Braids Pocahontas doll has extra long raven hair that can be styled many different ways with the enclosed pink and iridescent twister. *Pocahontas* wears a two-piece sky blue suede cloth fabric that is trimmed with iridescent and lilac colored fringe. Her jewelry is limited to her plastic blue choker with the white tooth. She comes with a sky blue hairbrush. The doll in this photo was made in Indonesia.

Disney characters © Disney Enterprises, Inc.

Disney characters © Disney Enterprises, Inc.

Disney's Pocahontas
Bead-So-Pretty Pocahontas
#14055 • 1995 • $30-40

Bead-So-Pretty Pocahontas doll is 18 inches tall. I have set my 11-½ inch doll next to her so that you can compare the sizes. This *Pocahontas* doll is wearing the exact same style dress as on *Sun Colors* and *Braided Beauty*, only her dress is solid bone colored suede cloth with copper colored fringe with a matching belt with plastic leaves on the ends. She comes with lots of beads and hair clips with ribbons and a beader-hook and a pistachio colored "Flit" hair-comb. The doll in this photo was made in China.

Disney characters © Disney Enterprises, Inc.

Disney characters © Disney Enterprises, Inc.

119

Disney's Pocahontas
Color Splash Hair Pocahontas
#14864 • 1995 • $15-25

Color Splash Hair Pocahontas doll is in a slim-line box. When exposed to sunlight her raven hair becomes black, turquoise and fuchsia colored. Mattel advises us not to expose this doll's hair to chlorine or intense heat for extended lengths of time, or the ability of her hair changing will be shortened. She wears a bone colored, one shoulder suede cloth dress with turquoise suede cloth fringe with two plastic leaves hanging from turquoise blue grosgrain ribbon. The doll in this photo was made in Indonesia. *Courtesy of Michelle Walker.*

Disney characters © Disney Enterprises, Inc.

Disney characters © Disney Enterprises, Inc.

POCAHONTAS

Disney characters © Disney Enterprises, Inc.

Disney characters © Disney Enterprises, Inc.

Disney's Pocahontas Color Splash Hair Nakoma
#14867 • 1995 • $15-25

Pocahontas Color Splash Hair Nakoma doll wears a two piece fuchsia and bone colored suede cloth fashion. Plastic butterflies hang from her skirt. She has a bone colored grosgrain ribbon in her hair and wears a pink choker. The doll in this photo was made in Indonesia.

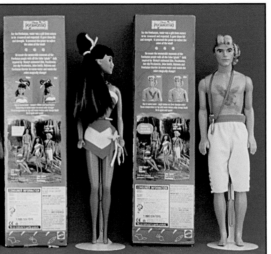

Disney characters © Disney Enterprises, Inc.

Disney's Pocahontas Color Splash Tattoo John Smith
#14865 • 1995 • $15-25

Pocahontas Color Splash Tattoo John Smith doll has an eagle on his chest. It is purple and changes to turquoise when placed in the sun. He wears bone colored pants with a turquoise suede cloth waistband. His only accessory is his compass, which hangs from his neck on a brown grosgrain ribbon. The doll in this photo was made in China.

Disney's Pocahontas
Color Splash Kocoum • No # • No Date • No Production

Color Splash Kocoum doll to my sad regret was never produced. I say sad because he would have made a great inexpensive doll to utilize with the American Indians from the *BARBIE®* Dolls of the World Series. You can see *Color Splash Kocoum* on the back of the *John Smith* doll's box. It may be difficult to see, but *John Smith's* box shows a sticker over what would have been *Kocoum's* name. Stickers were discontinued later and printed directly on the boxes were the words, "Powhatan Warrior Doll not available." This doll was never produced: hence no photo.

Disney characters © Disney Enterprises, Inc.

Disney's Pocahontas
Spirit of Love Gift Set • #14051 • 1995 • $25-35

Pocahontas Spirit of Love Gift Set was designed to signify *Pocahontas'* and *John Smith's* love for one another. *Pocahontas* with her tattooed arm wears a two piece strapless dress. It is made from a buff colored suede cloth with copper colored printed animals, leaves, birds and more. Her only accessory is the same style choker necklace that we have seen on the preceding dolls, except this time the tooth is a very pale shade of blue.

    John Smith doll wears a period piece shirt of suede cloth that is cinched at the waist with a navy blue leatherette belt with a brown bag stitched on it. His pants are sky blue suede cloth elastic pull-on. His boots are soft imitation leather in a wonderful rich shade of true blue. The dolls in this photo were made in China.

Disney characters © Disney Enterprises, Inc.

Disney characters © Disney Enterprises, Inc.

122

POCAHONTAS

Disney's Pocahontas
Feathers in the Wind
Special Edition
#14920 • 1996 • $40-50

Pocahontas Feathers in the Wind doll comes in a Velcro™ book box. It was originally sold at Toys R Us exclusively. There is good visibility to your doll, but book boxes take up twice as much room if you want to display your dolls openly without taking them out of the boxes. *Feathers in the Wind* is wearing a long pale peach dress with long sleeved and lots of fringe. Her belt is copper colored leatherette with turquoise, orange and black feathers that match the one's in her hair and on "Meeko's" Indian headdress. "Meeko" is hard plastic and he looks very mischievous. Notice "Flit" on *Pocahontas*' wrist— this one does not flutter. The doll is wearing the same choker as on all the other dolls and has the longest raven hair of all the *Pocahontas* dolls. She comes with her own *Pocahontas* signed saddle stand. The doll in this photo was made in China.

Disney characters © Disney Enterprises, Inc.

Disney characters © Disney Enterprises, Inc.

Disney characters © Disney Enterprises, Inc.

123

Disney's Pocahontas
Pocahontas Journey to a New World
#A19621 • 1998 • Not Produced

Pocahontas Journey to a New World doll was offered in the Mattel catalog, but it was cancelled in the summer of 1998 and never reached the marketplace. *Photo courtesy of Mattel, Inc.*

POCAHONTAS

Disney characters © Disney Enterprises, Inc.

Disney's Pocahontas
Flutter 'n Flower FLIT • #13492 • 1995 • $15-24

Pocahontas "Flutter 'n Flit" the hummingbird's iridescent wings flutter when you push his back feet. You can put him in his flower stand when he is sleepy. The hummingbird in this photo was made in China.

Disney's Pocahontas
Run 'n Carry MEEKO • #13491 • 1995 • $15-22

Pocahontas "Run 'n Carry Meeko," the raccoon, scampers across smooth surfaces. With a twist of his tail he picks up a cluster of molded colored plastic food and will run off with it. The raccoon in this photo was made in China.

Disney's Pocahontas
Sleep 'n Eat PERCY
#13490 • 1995 • $15-22

Pocahontas "Sleep 'n Eat Percy," the dog, closes his eyes and lies down when you press down on his head. When you press on his tail he sits up. His accessories include a gold-trimmed purple dog blanket and a yellow crown that when turned upside down becomes a dog bowl and has a bone molded inside. The dog in this photo was made in China.

Disney characters © Disney Enterprises, Inc.

POCAHONTAS

Disney's Pocahontas
Dress 'n Play Fashions • #68452 • No Date • $8-12

Pocahontas "Dress 'n Play Fashions" were presented in flat packs. All four fashions shared the same stock number as they were sold by the assortment. However, each had it's own name. They were called "Swimming," "Wilderness," "Winter," and "Dance Dress 'n Play." Each had a variety of Indian accessories that are lots of fun to play with and which work well with the Powhatan Village Playset. ARCOTOYS, INC., a Mattel company, made the fashions in China. *Courtesy of Michelle Walker.*

Disney characters © Disney Enterprises, Inc.

Disney characters © Disney Enterprises, Inc.

Disney characters © Disney Enterprises, Inc.

126

POCAHONTAS

Disney characters © Disney Enterprises, Inc.

Disney's Pocahontas
Earth Dance Fashion • #68541 • No Date • $6-8

Pocahontas "Earth Dance Fashions" came in four different colors. Three of the fashions had a one-piece dress, while the forth had a two piece dress. Each flat pack came with a fashion, a purse and a pair of moccasins. All four fashions shared the same stock number as they were sold by the assortment. ARCOTOYS, INC., a Mattel company, made the fashions in China. *Courtesy of Michelle Walker.*

Disney's Pocahontas
Powhatan Village Playset
#67217 • No Date • $25-35

Pocahontas Powhatan Village Playset has so many wonderful pieces that I prefer that you look at the photo, rather than read an extensive list. What you see is what you get, although colors may vary. The Village playset in this photo was made in China.

Disney characters © Disney Enterprises, Inc.

SLEEPING BEAUTY

Disney characters © Disney Enterprises, Inc.

Disney characters © Disney Enterprises, Inc.

Disney's Sleeping Beauty
Disney Classsics Sleeping Beauty • #4567 • 1991 • $45-50

Sleeping Beauty doll was the second in the series of "Classics" that Disney and Mattel worked on together. There were two different satin bodices for *Sleeping Beauty*, *Princess Aurora*. One was princess pink and the other has hot pink. The dark pink was a later release. Her floor length skirt is princess chiffon with "pixie dust." Both the bodices have white iridescent long sleeves and collar and the skirt has the same iridescent peplum. Both bodices reverse from pink to cadet blue while the skirt reverses to pale blue chiffon. *Sleeping Beauty* doll has a golden crown and matching necklace. Her accessories include a Little Little Golden Book, a pop-up character and an applicator, which you dampen with warm water to make her sleeping eyes open. Included in my package but not listed on the box were instructions and two additional pop-ups. You also get a pink hairbrush and white closed-toe shoes. The *Sleeping Beauty* storybook was made in the U.S.A. The dolls in these photos were made in China.

Disney characters © Disney Enterprises, Inc.

Disney's Sleeping Beauty
Disney Classics Prince Phillip
#4597 • 1991 • $90-100

Prince Phillip doll is not only handsome but gallant as well. You get a lot for your money with this doll. His costume is very versatile. When dressed as a Prince, he wears a regal red faux suede hat with a golden feather. His red detachable cape ties at the neck and has golden "pixie dust" printed on it. His shirt is the same blue satin as *Sleeping Beauty's* and has a wide golden ribbon belt. The puff part of his sleeves is striped red chiffon and the tapered parts of his sleeves are silver gray nylon, which match his pants. His pull-on boots are black suede cloth. His accessories include a silver colored plastic sword known as the Sword of Truth and the Shield of Virtue that is designed with blue metallic which accents his satin shirt.

  When you initially look at the *Prince Phillip* doll through the cello window of his package you do not realize the extraordinary amount of extra goodies you get. Underneath his Prince outfit he wears his horseman's outfit. In the picture on the left you see the Prince has a long-sleeve black nylon shirt with a high collar. In addition to this he has a chamois V-neck sleeveless vest. You also get two pop-up characters. The dolls in this photo were made in Malaysia.

Disney characters © Disney Enterprises, Inc.

Disney characters © Disney Enterprises, Inc.

SLEEPING BEAUTY

Disney Classics Sleeping Beauty
Sleeping Beauty Peasant Dress
#4614 • 1991 • $35-40

Sleeping Beauty "Peasant Dress" is two tone turquoise. The sleeves are a couple of shades lighter than the skirt, which is flocked with pixie dust. The white collar is stiff cotton. Her vest is black suede cloth. Her accessories include a black elastic hair ribbon and pop-up characters. There is a straw basket trimmed with turquoise topstitching, with multi green chiffon. The package states that there are berries included, but they are not, in fact it is a white cloth with red berries printed on it. Her shoes are black flats. This fashion in this photo was made in China.

Disney characters © Disney Enterprises, Inc.

Disney characters © Disney Enterprises, Inc.

Disney Classics Sleeping Beauty
Maleficent
Mask & Costume Playset
#4613 • 1991 • $40-45

"*Maleficent* Mask & Costume" was scarce even when it was available direct from Mattel. I would classify this as very hard to find. *Maleficent*'s mask is separate from her dress. It easily slips over the head of any 11-1/2 inch doll. Her dress is ominously black and has panels of rose pink that are embellished with pixie dust. There is purple ribbon down the front to match the purple chiffon sleeves and collar. She carries a gold colored plastic staff and comes with pop-up characters. Her shoes are black closed-toe pumps. This was the last piece released for the "Disney Classic *Sleeping Beauty* Collection." The fashion in this photo was made in China.

Disney characters © Disney Enterprises, Inc.

Disney characters © Disney Enterprises, Inc.

SLEEPING BEAUTY

Disney characters © Disney Enterprises, Inc.

Walt Disney's Sleeping Beauty
Sparkle Eyes Sleeping Beauty • #15808 • 1996 • $35-45

Sparkle Eyes Sleeping Beauty doll's beautiful gown is soft pink. Her collar is iridescent to match the bodice of her dress and the peplum. The sleeves are chiffon with golden glitter to match her full circle skirt. The hard plastic golden crown she wears is elegant in it's simplicity and matches her choker. She comes with a pink plastic hairbrush and has matching shoes. *Sparkle Eyes Sleeping Beauty* was a Disney Park and Disney Store exclusive. The doll in this photo was made in China.

Disney characters © Disney Enterprises, Inc.

Disney characters © Disney Enterprises, Inc.

Walt Disney's Sleeping Beauty
Wedding Sleeping Beauty
#18057 • 1997 • $75-85

Wedding Sleeping Beauty doll was an elusive exclusive for Toys R Us and it was the second in the series. The first was *Wedding Cinderella*, see page 50. This is the first time we see this face mold on a *Sleeping Beauty* doll. She is enclosed in a golden "pixie dusted" book box. The bodice of her wedding gown is iridescent brocade with solid satin at the collar, cuffs and peplum. There are two iridescent bows with two pastel pink rosettes on each shoulder that match her bouquet. The collar, front and waistline are trimmed with imitation seed pearls. Her skirt is white glittered chiffon over satin. Her veil is soft white chiffon with an iridescent fabric tiara. She wears imitation white plastic pearl-drop earrings, a choker and a white button ring. Included with this *Sleeping Beauty* is a white plastic hairbrush and white closed-toe pumps. The doll in this photo was made in Indonesia.

Disney characters © Disney Enterprises, Inc.

Disney characters © Disney Enterprises, Inc.

Disney characters © Disney Enterprises, Inc.

133

SLEEPING BEAUTY

Disney characters © Disney Enterprises, Inc.

Walt Disney's Sleeping Beauty
Signature Collection Sleeping
Beauty
40th Anniversary
#21712 • 1999 • $75-85
Photo courtesy of Mattel.

Disney characters © Disney Enterprises, Inc.

Walt Disney's Sleeping Beauty
Princess Stories Collection
Sleeping Beauty
#18192 • 1997 • $25-35

Sleeping Beauty Princess Stories doll is one of five Stories dolls. She is the hardest of them to find. Originally Mattel offered this doll packed six to a carton; few shopkeepers ever got six *Sleeping Beauty* dolls. Shortly into production Mattel changed the packaging to an assortment and included only one *Sleeping Beauty*. Therefore, she is hard to find. Mattel has used the same basic pattern for all the *Sleeping Beauty* dolls to date, but do change colors and fabrics. *Princess Stories Sleeping Beauty's* gown has the same large iridescent bodice, collar and peplum. The sleeves and skirt are pink nylon with a built in crinoline. She comes with a *Sleeping Beauty Little Little Golden Book*, the same gold crown and choker as on *Sparkle Eyes* from 1996. There is a darling little plastic magic "Merryweather" figurine included along with a pearl-like hairbrush and matching closed toe pumps. The doll in this photo was made in China.

134

SLEEPING BEAUTY

Walt Disney's Sleeping Beauty
Maleficent
Great Villains Collection
40th Anniversary
#20990 • 1999 • $75-85
Photo courtesy of Mattel.

SNOW WHITE & THE SEVEN DWARFS

Walt Disney's
Snow White and the Seven Dwarfs
Snow White
#37783 • 1992 • $40-50

Snow White and the Seven Dwarfs doll has more included in the package than one sees through the box cello. *Snow White* is wearing a village dress that is hidden by her gown. (See the photo on the right.) The bodice of the rag dress is utilized as the top for her floor length dress. The rag dress has white sleeves and collar, a royal blue bodice with white ribbon down the front. The skirt is powder blue nylon with a rag-cut hemline. The floor length gown has detachable blue, pink and white sleeves that slip right over the white sleeves of the rag dress. The skirt is daffodil yellow with flocked "fairy dust" over a layer of daffodil satin. Her red nylon cape is detachable and matches the red ribbon in her hair. Included in her package is a *Snow White and the Seven Dwarfs* Little Little Golden Book, pop-up characters a yellow hairbrush and white closed-toe pumps with molded bows. The fashion on this doll in this photo was made in Indonesia. The doll in this photo was made in Malaysia.

Disney characters © Disney Enterprises, Inc.

Disney characters © Disney Enterprises, Inc.

Disney characters © Disney Enterprises, Inc.

SNOW WHITE & THE SEVEN DWARFS

Walt Disney's
Snow White and the Seven Dwarfs
Dance 'n Play Deluxe Gift Set
#10559 • 1993 • $45-55

Snow White and the Seven Dwarfs Dance and Play Gift Set comes with all the same things that are described with the *Snow White* doll and with the Stackable Dwarfs. (See page 136.) The *Snow White* doll in this photo was made in Malaysia and the Dwarfs were made in Thailand.

Disney characters © Disney Enterprises, Inc.

Disney characters © Disney Enterprises, Inc.

Disney characters © Disney Enterprises, Inc.

137

Disney characters © Disney Enterprises, Inc.

Walt Disney's
Snow White and the Seven Dwarfs
Dopey & Sneezy Stackable Dolls
#0611 • 1992 • $20-30

Dopey and *Sneezy* dolls are poured plastic and are only jointed at the shoulders. You will see them in later chapters in gift sets. All *Seven Dwarfs* were also sold individually but the only way you could obtain the royal and powder blue nylon cloak with golden braiding was to buy this set or the Dance 'n Play set. (See page 137.) *Dopey* stands on *Sneezy's* shoulders so that they could dance with *Snow White*. Also included in this package is one pop-up character. The dolls in this photo were made in Thailand.

Disney characters © Disney Enterprises, Inc.

Disney characters © Disney Enterprises, Inc.

Disney characters © Disney Enterprises, Inc.

Walt Disney's Snow White and the Seven Dwarfs
Seven Dwarfs Gift Set • #5278 • 1993 • $145-155

Snow White and the *Seven Dwarfs* Gift Set was available for all Mattel regular accounts to purchase. Although I do not have the individually sold *Dwarfs* to show you, you can see each of them clearly in this photo. All *Seven Dwarfs* are "color change" dolls. When either icy water or warm water is applied to these dolls something happens to them. 1) *Sleepy's* eyes close. 2) *Happy's* face gets dirty. 3) *Dopey* has a kiss appear on his cheek. 4) *Sneezy's* nose turns red. 5) *Grumpy's* eyebrows raise. 6) *Bashful's* face turns red. 7) *Doc* has a jewel in his hand that turns color. The dolls in this photo were made in Thailand.

Disney characters © Disney Enterprises, Inc.

Disney characters © Disney Enterprises, Inc.

Walt Disney's Snow White and the Seven Dwarfs
Snow White and the Seven Dwarfs Classic Gift Set • #10558 • 1993 • $185-200

Snow White and the *Seven Dwarfs* Classic Gift Set was only sold at one of the wholesale clubs. This gift set is rare. Some refer to this gift set as the deluxe gift set, but nowhere on the box does it say "deluxe." The *Dwarfs* in this set are also color change features. It came with all the same fashions and accessories described on the individual dolls on previous pages, except there is no cloak included. The *Dwarfs* in this set were made in Thailand. *Snow White* was made in Malaysia.

Walt Disney's
Snow White and the Seven Dwarfs
The Queen Mask & Costume Playset
#7784 • 1992 • $25-35

The *Queen* Mask & Costume Playset is hard to find. The *Queen*'s mask slips over any 11½ inch doll. Her mask and cape are one piece. The headdress is black nylon trimmed with raspberry colored nylon, the collar is iridescent fabric and her crown is detachable if you wish to snip the thread that holds it to her head. Her dress is a medieval style gown made of nylon. The sleeves are lavender. The bodice and skirt are purple and has "pixie dust" on the bodice. Her belt is red and golden braiding. She comes with pop-up characters which include a "magic mirror." The fashion in this photo was made in China.

Disney characters
© Disney
Enterprises, Inc.

Disney characters © Disney Enterprises, Inc.

SNOW WHITE & THE SEVEN DWARFS

Walt Disney's
Snow White and the Seven Dwarfs
Special Sparkles Collection Snow White
#11832 • 1994 • $30-40

Special Sparkles Snow White doll is named so, because her eyes actually sparkle. In fact, her whole dress sparkles. Mattel and Disney selected some wonderful fabric to dress this doll in. They utilized the exact same pattern for this dress as all the preceding photos show. But this time, the bodice is metallic blue with metallic red sleeves with sky blue iridescent puff sleeves. The skirt is floor length and loaded with extra glitter. Her collar is sparkly white and she has a red and golden ribbon in her hair. There is a yellow decal saddle stand that was made in Malaysia, a red hairbrush and yellow closed-toe pumps with molded bows. The box states that "the stand made was in either Malaysia or China as Marked." The doll in this photo was made in Malaysia.

Disney characters © Disney Enterprises, Inc.

Disney characters © Disney Enterprises, Inc.

Disney characters © Disney Enterprises, Inc.

Walt Disney's Snow White and the Seven Dwarfs
Happy Birthday Or Blanche-Neige et les Sept Nains Joyeux Anniversaire
#16535 • 1996 • $40-50

Snow White and the Seven Dwarfs Happy Birthday doll was to have been the first in a series of Disney princesses wearing birthday fashions. Three years have passed and I have not seen the second one yet. The box states that this was a Walmart Exclusive. The bodice on *Snow White's* dress has sheen to it. Her large white collar is iridescent on top and satin finish on the underside. Her puff sleeves are pink metallic and iridescent blue. Her underskirt is bright yellow. Her overskirt is also yellow with glittered illusion with blue and pink twisted iridescent ribbons streaming from the waistline. Included in her package are a plastic bunny, a doe, a cake and three party hats in three different sizes to fit the characters. You also get seven tiny stickers, you guessed right! *Seven Dwarfs*. Naturally, there is a matching yellow hairbrush and white plastic closed-toe pumps with molded bows. The doll in this photo was made in Malaysia.

Disney characters © Disney Enterprises, Inc.

Disney characters © Disney Enterprises, Inc.

Walt Disney's
Snow White and the Seven Dwarfs
Princess Stories Collection Snow White
#18194 • 1997 • $20-30

Snow White Princess Stories doll, (notice the *Seven Dwarfs* was not included in the title of this doll) as with all the Princess Stories Collection is very reasonably priced. *Snow White* has a red ribbon in her hair, white iridescent collar and a red cape. The bodice of this dress is royal blue with golden cord down the front. The sleeves are red chiffon and iridescent blue. Her skirt is canary yellow nylon with a white-netted crinoline with a ¼-inch cotton embroidered border. You get a Little Little Golden Book and a plastic bunny friend. Included in her package are a yellow hairbrush and yellow plastic close-toe pumps with molded bows. The Little Little Golden Book was made in U.S.A. The doll in this photo was made in China.

Disney characters © Disney Enterprises, Inc.

Disney characters © Disney Enterprises, Inc.

143

Disney characters © Disney Enterprises, Inc.

Walt Disney's
Snow White and the Seven Dwarfs
Wedding Snow White
#18958 • 1997 • $55-65

Snow White and the Seven Dwarfs Wedding Snow White doll is the third in the wedding series for Toys R Us. She is dressed in a candlelight satin finished gown with ivory colored satin rosettes on the bodice and skirt. There is candlelight colored illusion ruffle down the front of the bodice, which wraps gently around the back of her neck. Her puff sleeves are white threaded illusion. Her veil has a satin ribbon with three faux pearls at the top that is stitched to her hair. The back part of the veil is made of illusion while the front is made from white netting. Unfortunately the netting hides her big brown eyes. Her bouquet is made of multi colored flowers and is surrounded by the same illusion as the ruffle on the bodice of her dress. Her gloves are particularly unusual. They are also made from illusion, but are a different texture. Included in her book box is a plastic mother-of-pearl finished hairbrush and closed-toe pumps with molded bows and a signature saddle stand. The costume was made in Indonesia. The doll in this photo was made in Malaysia.

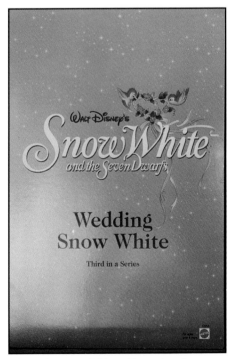

Disney characters © Disney Enterprises, Inc.

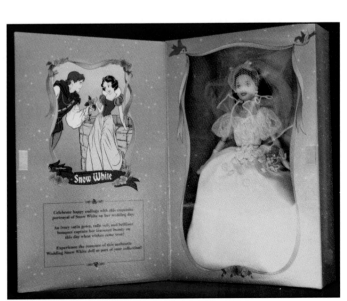

Disney characters © Disney Enterprises, Inc.

Walt Disney's Snow White and the Seven Dwarfs
The Signature Collection Snow White
Collector Edition
60th Anniversary
#17761 • 1997 • $75-80

Snow White and the Seven Dwarfs 60th Anniversary doll is elegant and simple. She was the second in the Signature Series, preceded by Signature *Belle*. The bodice of her gown is blue on blue brocade with golden beads around the neck and down the front which meet a golden braid at the waistline. The puff sleeves are red and blue satin with golden topstitching. The skirt is extraordinarily full in soft banana colored fabric that has the hand of silk charmeuse, but I think is synthetic. Underneath is the perfect white petticoat to make her skirt stand out. *Snow White* doll has a red satin ribbon in her hair. Included in the package is a sweet bird character and white decal saddle stand. Her shoes are pale yellow closed-toe pumps with real golden satin ribbon bows, not molded. The packaging is superb, unfortunately the photo loses much of the detail. The box is metallic candy apple red with flowers and birds sketched on it. This book box has a wonderful peek-a-boo window and a lovely pop out of *Snow White* with some of her favorite animal friends. The doll in this photo was made in Indonesia.

Disney characters © Disney Enterprises, Inc.

Disney characters © Disney Enterprises, Inc.

Disney characters © Disney Enterprises, Inc.

Disney characters © Disney Enterprises, Inc.

Disney characters © Disney Enterprises, Inc.

Disney characters © Disney Enterprises, Inc.

Walt Disney's Snow White and the Seven Dwarfs
Evil Queen • Fourth in the Great Villains Collection,
Limited Edition • #18626 • 1998 • $80-90

Snow White Evil Queen's face mold is slightly larger than the mold that was used for the costume. Her dress is made with much more expensive fabric and is more elaborately designed, as you saw on page 140. She is wearing a nylon skull cap, which hides her black shoulder length rooted hair. Her cape is trimmed with gold-tone braid and a button closure that resembles a ruby colored crystal ball. The cape is made from luxurious black rayon velvet with a red satin finished lining. The body of her purple dress is the same as her cape lining and has a golden threaded red belt with tassels. The Medieval sleeves are tone on tone leaf print and are trimmed with plain white satin to match her large stand-up collar. Her accessories include a pair of nylon gauntlets, a golden crown and matching closed-toe pumps. There is a red box with golden heart and dagger that has special detachable handles so that the *Evil Queen* can hold it in her hands. Also included in this package is a distinguished signature stand, a letter of authenticity and instructions. The doll in this photo was made in Indonesia. This is another gem designed by Mattel's Lisa Temming.

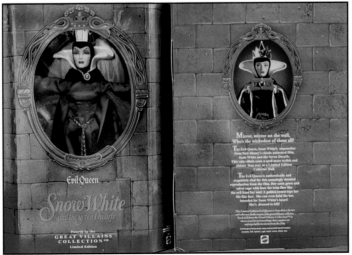

Disney characters © Disney Enterprises, Inc.

Disney characters © Disney Enterprises, Inc.

Disney Classics
Evil Queen
"Mirror, Mirror"
#None • 1998 • $8,500

Designed by Lisa Temming, Disney's *Snow White and the Seven Dwarfs Evil Queen* was a one-of-a-kind doll made for the 5th Anniversary for C.A.A.F.'s (Children Affected by Aids Foundation) on October 24, 1998. The costume was made of velvet trimmed with 24K gold braid and French chantilly lace and accessorized with a real jewel crown. It sold at auction for $8,500. *Photo courtesy of Mattel.*

Disney characters © Disney Enterprises, Inc.

Walt Disney's
Snow White and the Seven Dwarfs
Disney Classics
My Favorite Fairytale™ Collection
#21932 • 1998 • $18-22

My Favorite Fairytale Snow White doll is one of three in the series. The other two are *Alice in Wonderland* and *Cinderella*. (See pages 55 and 107). Each doll was assigned its own stock number. Stores could order the dolls by assortment. The stock number for the assortment was #22039. *Snow White* is wearing an all-satin blue gown. Her accessories include a red satin hair ribbon, yellow pumps with a molded bow, and a pink colored hairbrush. The doll comes with *Dopey* and a squirrel and rabbit animal friends stand-up clip art. The doll in this photo was made in China.

Disney characters © Disney Enterprises, Inc.

Clássicos Disney Branca de Neve
Branca de Neve • Estrela
No Stock # • No Date • $125

Clássicos Disney *Branca de Neve's* gown is intensely different from the American version of *Snow White*. The bodice is made of chalk-blue suede cloth with a crisscross printed bodice. The fabric of her cape is the same as *Prince Phillip's*. The red satin ribbon in her hair has a stitched-down bow. She has a plastic yellow button ring, and red shoes with yellow bows that the American *Snow White* does not have. To compare to the U.S. version, see page 137. The doll in this photo was made in Brazil. *Doll courtesy of Bob Gardner.*

Disney characters © Disney Enterprises, Inc.

Disney characters © Disney Enterprises, Inc.

Disney characters © Disney Enterprises, Inc.

Clássicos Disney A Bela Adormecida
Bela Adomecida • Estrela
#504453 • No date • $125

Clássicos Disney *A Bela Adormecida's* gown is the exact same pattern as the American version of Sleeping Beauty. The rectangle bodice, however, is not satin, it is acetate. Her crown is very plain, whereas ours is textured. She comes with a rectangle cut sponge raher than an applicator. To compare the U.S. version, see page 128. The doll in this photo was made in Brazil. *Doll courtesy of Bob Gardner.*

Disney characters © Disney Enterprises, Inc.

Disney characters © Disney Enterprises, Inc.

Disney characters © Disney Enterprises, Inc.

Disney characters © Disney Enterprises, Inc.

Clássicos Disney Adormecida
Príncipe Felipe • Estrela
#504469 • No date • $95

Clássicos Disney Adormecida *Príncipe Felipe*, when comparing to the American version of Prince Phillip, probably has the most obvious differences. First, his hair is tan, not brown. Secondly, his shirt is acetate, not satin; thirdly, his puff sleeves do not have glitter; his pants are grey, not tan. The back of the boxes for both *Sleeping Beauty* and *Felipe* are the same. To compare to the U.S version, see page 129. The doll in this photo was made in Brazil. *Doll courtesy of Bob Gardner.*

Disney characters © Disney Enterprises, Inc.

Disney characters © Disney Enterprises, Inc.

Clássicos Disney Aladdin
Aladdin • Estrela
#505016 • No Date • $75

Clássicos Disney *Aladdin* made by Estrela in Brazil, at first glance appears to be identical to the American version of *Aladdin*. There are actually a few minor differences. First this is not a gift set, there is no extra fashion, secondly the golden trim is a different texture, thirdly the jewel on his turban is a pale pink verses a deep ruby color and fourthly there is no "Abu" monkey. To compare to the U.S. version, see page 4. The doll in this photo was made in Brazil. *Doll courtesy of Bob Gardner.*

Disney characters © Disney Enterprises, Inc.

Disney characters © Disney Enterprises, Inc.

Disney characters © Disney Enterprises, Inc.

Disney characters © Disney Enterprises, Inc.

Disney Aladdin
Jasmine • Estrela
No Stock # • No Date • $75

Disney Aladdin *Jasmine* doll, in her slim-line box is basically the same as our *Water Jewel Jasmine* doll from 1993. Estrela did not believe in putting dates on the boxes because they felt the dolls would have a longer shelf life, which would result in a longer selling time. The pattern of the *Jasmine's* costume is the same as the American version, however the fabric is very different. To compare to the U.S. version, see page 8. The doll in this photo was made in Brazil. *Doll courtesy of Bob Gardner.*

Disney characters ©
Disney Enterprises, Inc.

Disney characters
© Disney
Enterprises, Inc.

Disney characters © Disney Enterprises, Inc.

Clássicos Disney A Bela e a Fera
Fera Prince • Estrela
#505856 • No Date • $95

Clássicos Disney *A Bela e a Fera* Prince is wearing cotton socks, where as in the American version of the *Prince* and the *Beast* wears nylon ones. The hair on the Prince is several shades lighter and is much softer than both the American and German dolls. The *Beast* costume is a brighter royal blue and the *Beast*'s mane is extremely fine and silk-like. To compare to the U.S. version, see page 21. The doll in this photo was made in Brazil. *Doll courtesy of Bob Gardner.*

Disney characters © Disney Enterprises, Inc.

Disney characters © Disney Enterprises, Inc.

Clássicos Disney Cinderela
Cinderela • Estrela
#505344 • No Date • $125

Clássicos Disney *Cinderela*, spelled with one "L" by Estrela in Brazil is extremely different than the American version of *Cinderella*. Estrela's *Cinderela*'s gown is not made from satin; it has the hand of acetate. It has paisleys with glitter. The peplum and sleeves are chiffon and lightly glittered while the bodice is plain. This *Cinderela* has iridescent gauntlets instead of nylon gloves. Her hair is made from a satiny fiber. The back of the boxes for both *Cinderela* and *Príncipe Encantado* are the same. To compare to the U.S. version, see page 40. The doll in this photo was made in Brazil. *Doll courtesy of Bob Gardner.*

Disney characters © Disney Enterprises, Inc.

Disney characters © Disney Enterprises, Inc.

Disney characters © Disney Enterprises, Inc.

Disney characters © Disney Enterprises, Inc.

Clássicos Disney Cinderelá Príncipe Encantado • Estrela
#505351 • No Date • $125

Clássicos Disney *Príncipe Encantado's* costume is less ornate than the American version of *Prince Charming*, although our doll's costume is pictured the same on the back of the box. His epaulettes, ribbons and belt are plain. The pillow that *Cinderela's* shoe is sitting on is more turquoise in color and is a soft satin, whereas the American version is lighter blue and quilted. This doll's red pants are trimmed with a different golden braid and are made from a much stiffer fabric. Included in this package is a pair of sheer nylon socks and paper cutouts. To compare to the U.S. version, see page 41. The doll in this photo was made in Brazil. *Doll courtesy of Bob Gardner.*

Disney characters © Disney Enterprises, Inc.

Disney characters © Disney Enterprises, Inc.

Disney characters © Disney Enterprises, Inc.

Die Schone und das Biest
Disney Classics
Das Biest • Germany
#2436 • 1992 • $125

Disney Classics *Das Biest* is basically the same doll and costume as the American version of the *Prince* and the *Beast*. The back of the box reads Euro Disney and shows two characters that we don't see on the U.S.A. package. The liner has an interesting forest scene behind the doll and mask. Both the doll and the fashion are the same as the American version. The *Prince* comes with a golden plastic hairbrush, magical mirror, and a comb. To compare to the U.S. version, see page 21. The doll in this photo was made in Malaysia. *Doll courtesy of Bob Gardner.*

For more foreign Disney *BARBIE®* dolls please refer to Volume II.

Disney characters © Disney Enterprises, Inc.

156